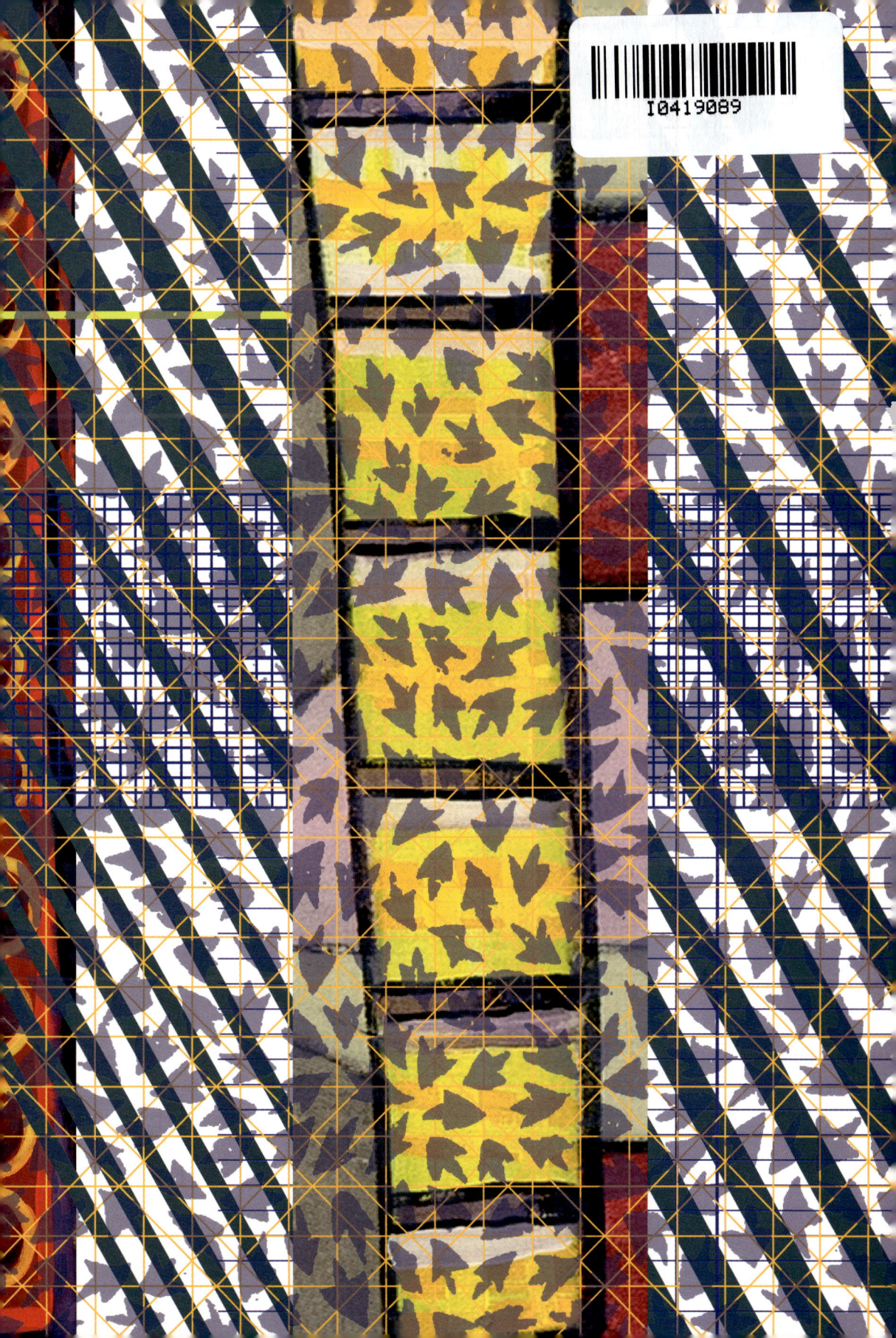

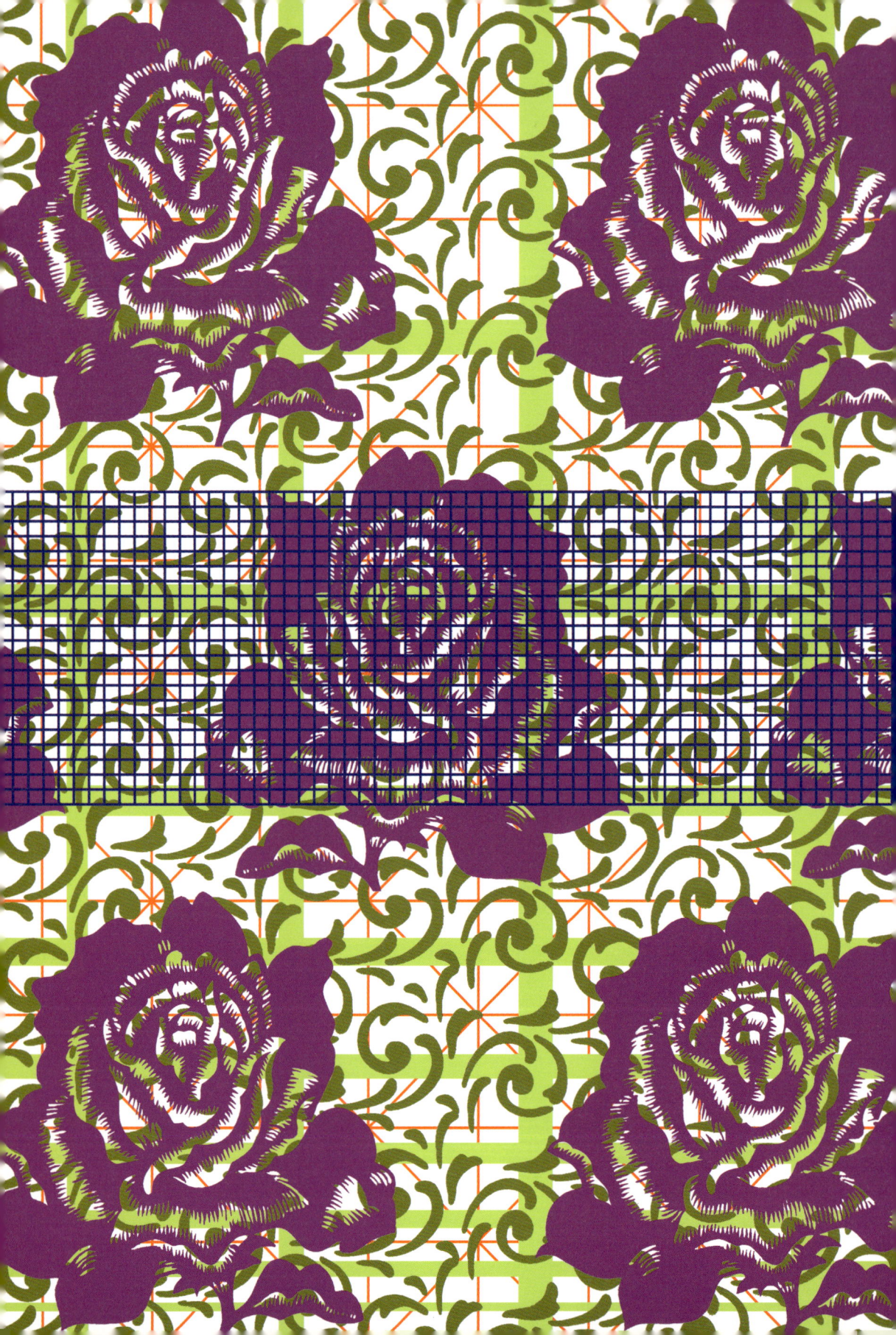

5

7 **Introduction**
Amy Tobin

8 **There is a history
that I know to be true**
Amy Tobin

38 **Lubaina and Magda and
Zofia and Nina and**
Amelia Groom

49 **How Can I Help You?**
Lubaina Himid

61 **Letter to Magda**
Lubaina Himid

66 **Letter to Magda**
Aneta Krzemień

73 **List do Magdy**
Aneta Krzemień

82 **Letter to Zofia**
Lubaina Himid

86 **Letter to Nina**
Lubaina Himid

102 **Postcard to Aneta**
Magda Stawarska

103 **Postcard to Lubaina**
Magda Stawarska

105 **Afterword**
Andrew Nairne and Amy Tobin

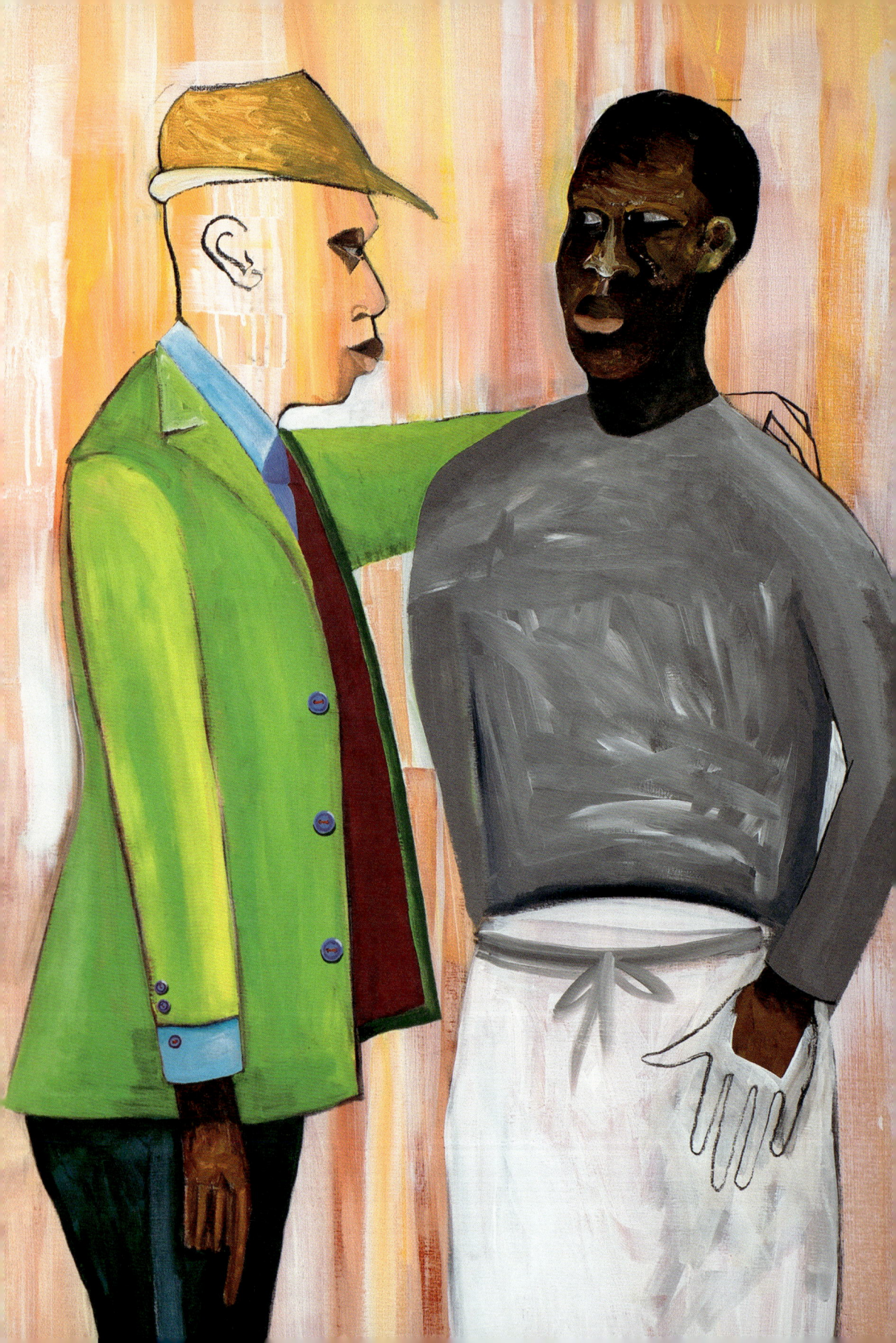

Introduction

Amy Tobin

This publication accompanies Lubaina Himid and Magda Stawarska's exhibition *Another Chance Encounter* at Kettle's Yard, Cambridge. It records three bodies of work split across two galleries and installed in the historic Kettle's Yard house, which was once home to H.S. Jim and Helen Ede. While Himid and Stawarska's additions to the house activate its spaces directly, the installations *How Can I Help You?* and *Slightly Bitter* also engage with the Edes and the foundation of the Kettle's Yard house and collection.

Himid's paintings, grouped together under the title *How Can I Help You?*, offer glimpses of interactions between shopkeepers and their customers. Centring incidental, everyday scenes these five paintings draw close attention to the relationships between ten men, as they negotiate each other. Unlike most figurative paintings, which tend to make clear the identities of their subjects, these 'minor' scenes invite uncertainty and curiosity. Full of Himid's characteristic vibrant colour and pattern, these paintings also incorporate motifs from the Kettle's Yard collection, bringing the world of Kettle's Yard's founders Jim and Helen Ede into Himid's orbit.

Stawarska and Himid's installation *Slightly Bitter* originated with the little-known correspondence between the writer Zofia Gaudier-Brzeska and the artist Nina Hamnett.[1] Exchanged between 1917 and 1918, the letters trace the two women's efforts to navigate their own complex relationship and to secure the artistic legacy of Henri Gaudier-Brzeska following his early death in 1915 during World War I. Henri Gaudier-Brzeska's estate, including his art and archive, was foundational to what became the Kettle's Yard collection. With this installation, Himid and Stawarska elaborate on lives usually kept at the margins of the story of Kettle's Yard and modern art more broadly.

The exhibition, and this publication, stage a series of conversations and encounters, bringing together distinct, ordinary and perhaps minor histories and feelings to trouble what is known and understood. Essays written by myself and by Amelia Groom speculate on the resonant political potential of the stories opened up by Himid and Stawarska's work, while the artists along with the writer Aneta Krzemień have contributed a series of scripts, fictions, letters and notes exploring their encounters with one another and other protagonists, named and unnamed.

Another chance encounter is the ruling logic here: it registers no fatigue, but the strange reality that history is made of ordinary, everyday and serendipitous moments.

---

1   We use the variation 'Zofia' to refer to the writer usually known as Sophie Gaudier-Brzeska in English language publications in recognition of her own naming practices and the mulitlinguism of this project.

Amy Tobin

Lubaina Himid has noted her love of Kettle's Yard a few times in voice and in print. In 1995 she wrote that 'After hours and years of looking at paintings at Kettle's Yard in Cambridge and from the letters of Frances Hodgkins recently read, I am not surprised to find that I long to sit and stare out from a stone house high above the waves and marvel at the light and the warmth and the great distance from London'.[2] Sat in the house itself in 2025, she said: 'I've been talking about Kettle's Yard forever. I've modelled places I've lived on this house. [...] It says so much to me about British art: its brownness, its greyness, its impossibility. It's so fantastically difficult for me to paint in the way the works are here, and I love the way that everywhere there are rugs clearly from somewhere else, from North Africa. There is light, but no windows. You could be anywhere.'[3]

But Kettle's Yard hasn't always loved Himid. Her archive holds a series of notes towards an application to the 1997–98 artist residency scheme. In a list of pros and cons, presumably written to help with decision making, she notes: 'Yes: rest from teaching, op[portunity] to paint a lot, new environment, exhibition at K[ettle's] Y[ard]' and under 'No': 'lectures, workshops, Cambridge, academic life, [...] 2 refs, – who?'.[4] In a subsequent folder, the finished application letter (and copious CV) appears:

> Dear panel,
>
> During the last ten years using a variety of media including watercolour, film, wooden cut outs and painted canvas I have attempted to rewrite history even when it was unfashionable.
>
> Essentially, I am a history painter. I have remade great and not so great paintings in order to posit a satirical and sometimes political point.
>
> There is a history that I know to be true but which is not recorded: I invent where I please.
>
> The main concerns of my work have been black history and black strategy. Usually the audience is invited through the work to discourse around the black woman artist's position as central to cultural production. An in depth knowledge of world politics and black cultural history simply adds to the enjoyment and to the discussion: it is not essential.
>
> Always there is colour vibrancy human movement and narrative. Usually there is a challenge to unravel chaos and connections.

During my residency at Kettle's Yard I would like to investigate architecture, ritual and conversation. All these are subjects I have tackled before but not in the context of this particular microcosm. I hope to use the buildings and the geography of the town itself to make work about absence and presence, about the establishment and fixing of ideas and the possibility of change. I hope this gives you some idea of my work and I hope to be able to discuss it further with you in person.

Lubaina Himid[5]

The letter of rejection follows later in the file.

We could invent a story of what might have happened on this residency, postulating which rituals would have been investigated, which clues and connections unravelled and which ideas unfixed.

Perhaps Himid would have addressed home, the modernist still life or interior scene, revisiting some of the thinking she had done in collaboration with the curator Jill Morgan, when both were working at Touchstones, Rochdale a decade earlier. She might have reworked a college dinner table into a stage for strategising, or created a new series of portraits of figures absent from history for a college hall. Or maybe something would have begun from the maritime paintings of Alfred Wallis and Christopher Wood, building on Himid's reimaginings of sea and shore.

The sea has been a major theme of her work, taking in the personal experience of migration by boat from Zanzibar to London as an infant, along with childhood summers on Blackpool beach, and sea-gazing during visits back to Zanzibar as an adult, in full knowledge of the world historical significance of the ocean as a conduit for enslavement and colonial expansion. Himid's seas are sometimes seen through the windows of seemingly institutional settings, recognising the often unacknowledged presence of those pasts in the structures we live and work within. Elsewhere in Himid's work, the sea moves from background to foreground. Since the painting *Two Shores* (1989) to the major bodies of work *Beach House* (1995), *Plan B* (1999/2000), *Zanzibar* (1999–2023) and *Le Rodeur* (2015–16), it has been a persistent texture that stands in for the brutal remapping of social relations in the violence of colonial extraction.

'Where life is precious, life is precious' is the axiom of the Marxist geographer Ruth Wilson Gilmore.[6] Gilmore is one of the core strategists of the prison abolition movement in the United States, although her theories and commitments resonate internationally. Abolitionism is about social transformation toward freedom. Fundamentally, this includes the call to 'decarcerate', or to abolish prisons and the broader system of criminalisation, but Gilmore has sought a more expansive practice of abolition, what she calls 'life in rehearsal'.[7] The movement of abolition then, is not only about breaking down specific structures – built, institutional, social and psychic – but making new relations. She says we must recognise 'how interpersonal abolition must be', referring to the ways in which the dynamics of power, vulnerability and dehumanisation that the carceral system produces and reproduces, can only be undone by establishing our 'radical dependency' on one another to preserve and enrich life.[8] 'Where life is precious, life is precious' is a blueprint for a future to be worked on in the present, but also a damning indictment of a present still resonating with the violence of the past.[9]

Recently, I listened to an interview with Gilmore in which she described how she came to geography late, and with a drama degree.[10] At first, she joked at the discontinuity, before connecting theatre and geography as practices of world making, which both involve people, things and environments coming together. She goes on to say that political organising, or 'organising ourselves with one another and the environment' is the work of placemaking. It is in making these new places, which are always ways of being together, that we can transform reality. If the relations change then so must the architectures, spaces and structures that accommodate us. One of Gilmore's books is simply titled *Change Everything*.[11] Lubaina Himid has a mantra: 'How do you spell change?'[12]

Most accounts of Himid's career begin with her training in theatre design, rather than fine art, at Wimbledon College of Art. She has said this is where she learnt to collaborate, because unlike the artist's studio calibrated for the isolated and original genius, theatre designers must learn to work with others, even if they still want to believe they are in charge.[13] Magda Stawarska is one of Himid's closest collaborators. They began their work together when Himid requested Stawarska's aid in remastering the audio of the major installation *Naming the Money* (2004), before revisiting other past bodies of work and making them new. A key example is *Zanzibar* (1999–2023), a collaborative installation based on a series of a nine paintings that Himid first made after a return visit to the country of her birth, a former British 'protectorate', in 1997. Comprised of refracting abstractions, diamond patterns and long drips of paint, Himid has said that the initial works are 'paintings of cloves, of rain, of closed

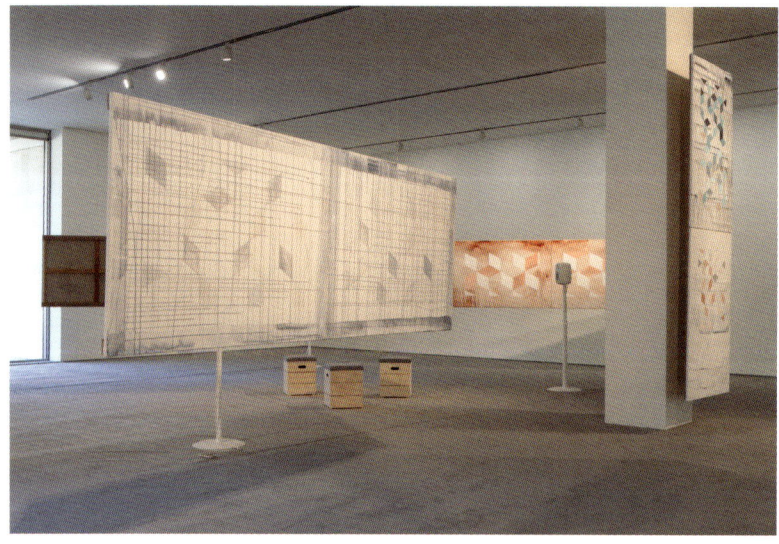

Lubaina Himid
and Magda
Stawarska,
Zanzibar,
Installation
view, 1999-2023

shutters; [...] paintings of the sea, fishing nets, death from malaria and of course women's tears'. They confront the place of her birth and – as the site of her father's early death – memories of tragedy, displacement and non-belonging negotiated through her mother and her return to England.[14] Although first displayed at Mostyn, Llandudno in 1999, Himid set about revisiting this series – an example of what Dorothy Price has called Himid's 'painterly autoethnography' – in collaboration with Stawarska, who composed an accompanying libretto, and freed the paintings from the gallery walls to hang in space.[15]

Stawarska's composition unfolds over forty minutes and eight channels, braiding sounds of rainfall and weather reports with accounts from guidebooks of Zanzibar, commentary on British lifestyles of the 1950s gleaned from BBC radio programmes, oud music, arias and Himid's voice. Composed over time and from intimate conversations between the two artists, this soundwork brings the ordinary and the ubiquitous together with the grand drama of both the Zanzibarian Taarab style and Western opera. A lifelong opera fan, Himid has said that 'the history of painting makes it very difficult to do what you can do in opera' to show women working through heartbreak and loss.[16] If painting cannot always 'communicate something important' that 'you didn't know how to do' then a composer like Stawarska can 'make a layered song'. As Omar Kholeif has written of Zanzibar: 'Stawarska engraves Himid's memories', summoning a picture of life between and without, from a collective chorus of voice and sound.'[17]

Here Stawarska's capacity to listen, 'hovering', as she has described it, creates the possibility of relating from a position of complex impressionism.[18] Not claiming space, but gathering and accumulating, Stawarska's work is a form of placemaking through attentiveness to people, spaces and things. In the ordinary dailiness of practices informing and converging, as well as in the intense commitment to one another's histories and artistic experiment, Himid and Stawarska's collaboration asks us to engage in something richer beyond the exceptional singularity of the artist or artwork.

*

If Himid had been an artist-in-residence at Kettle's Yard in 1997, perhaps she would have turned her attention to the carpets in the house as she has in 2025 for *Another Chance Encounter*.

Himid's painting *Flying Carpet*, one of a series of new works made for the Kettle's Yard house, occupies the space on the high wall of the double-height void at the centre of Leslie Martin and David Owers' design for the 1970 extension. Taking the space previously occupied by a large and heavy hanging textile, this work is a blend of rug-like or textile-pattern passages of paint and blocks or strokes of abstract colour. These patches sometimes appear to be stitched together by painted yellow or pink sutures. Their scales shift so drastically from the minute to the gigantic that we seem to be looking into a deep dimensional space of moving planes.

Some sections directly reference the colours and patterns of textiles in the Kettle's Yard house. For instance, the passages of stripes evoke the rug woven in the Atlas Mountains that sits on a bench in the cottages, while the patterned border around the whole painting is reminiscent of the Zemmour carpets common to central Morocco. There are also references to textiles from Himid's personal collection, including the bulbous petal flowers from an East African kanga that also bloom on her *Man in a Swiss Army Drawer* (2025) on display in the nearby dining table drawer. This in turn resonates with the rose, taken from another much cherished kanga, that Himid has painted directly on the wall of a cupboard in the Kettle's Yard cottages for her work *Saving It For Later* (2025). Stawarska has also taken up this motif, printing it onto her own drawer work *Cytrony* (2025), which also depicts the rarely seen Kettle's Yard kitchen, the location of her soundwork *Sweet Sharp Taste of Limes* (2025). This tangle of motifs – which also extends into the works in the galleries – is the visible trace of the exchange of ideas and feelings between the two artists who also share a life.

The rose, hand painted by Himid over and over again across many works, is printed by Stawarska in *Cytrony* in a pattern that seems to make them dance across the plane. If, as Himid has suggested, textiles and patterns can provide a feeling of recognition, comfort and sanctuary, then at Kettle's Yard the repeated rose entwines Himid and Stawarska into the house.[19] Their almost-presence is literalised in *Sweet Sharp Taste of Limes*, with the combination of Magda chopping, stirring and brewing coffee while Lubaina reads Audre Lorde's poem 'On a Night of the Full Moon', conjuring images of love and desire amid the everyday: 'your lips quick as young birds / between your thighs the sweet / sharp taste of limes'.[20]

Himid and Stawarska's tenancy of the Kettle's Yard house enlivens it, inviting us to imagine everyday activities and sounds in an otherwise static space. Far from a disruptive intervention, these works subtly reveal things hidden or downplayed. For instance, the bright purple radio in *Flying Carpet* – painted, Himid has said, to summon sound into the work – evokes the Edes' hidden record player sunk into a nearby wooden chest.[21] These works lay a claim on Kettle's Yard, not only reviving its lived qualities, but also insisting on a new presence. This is an invitation to see the house and collection from different, though nonetheless integral, vantage points, shifting the focus from the idiosyncrasy of Jim and Helen Ede's founding renovation, building and placement, to see Kettle's Yard within the longer trajectory of their own lives, and the domestic aspirations of early twentieth century modernism, as well as speculating on other possible residents and custodians.

While we know that the Edes gifted Kettle's Yard to the University of Cambridge to ensure its preservation in 1966, seven years before they gave up residence, works like *Man in a Swiss Army Drawer* invite us to imagine other potential occupants. Part of a longer series of artworks on found objects (often drawers and doors), in which Himid summons presences of unknown, often male, characters, this work offers a portrait of a Kettle's Yard resident in the fragmented remains of an everyday, odds-and-ends drawer. His face is painted in profile and augmented by the kanga flower motif, a stamp, tape and the metallic red wrapper of a chocolate made by Victorix, the manufacturers famous for their Swiss army knife. The collage is an image of ordinary life, even if the implications of another resident of this very special home are anything but.

These new, imaginary tenants are not foreign to Kettle's Yard. They remind us of the Edes' commitment to hospitality across their lives, and homes. Perhaps most important to this history is the period in which they lived in Tangier, Morocco between 1936 and 1952, when the coastal city was an International Zone under the joint administration of France, Spain, the United Kingdom and Italy.[22] Between 1946 and 1947, the Edes hosted British servicemen stationed on nearby Gibraltar for weekend retreats in their home Whitestone, designed and built to conjure rooms 'filled with sky'.[23] Keen to offer these men hospitality, Jim Ede wrote: 'It is our intention to give the service man exactly what we would give to any of our personal friends; to give him the best we have'.[24]

The Kettle's Yard archive holds an extensive record of these visits, written by Ede under the titles 'Variations on a Weekend Theme', and 'Tangier log'.[25] Conducted like an experiment, Ede documented the visits of 400 servicemen over the two year period. Each account is a little portrait of variously rowdy, studious or charming characters, usually white, some clearly adept to the Edes' beautiful bohemianism, others awed at the wealth and privilege (no class positions are recorded), their group dynamic and the various activities undertaken, including lunches, dinners, dancing, shopping and visits to Spartel beach. The resulting 'Tangier Log', to borrow the associations of the alternate title 'Variations on a Weekend Theme', is akin to a composition: with the weekend visit, its meals and compulsory beach trip, forming the basic structure against which the vitality of young lives, passions and relationships play out. Whitestone was a chance to deviate from the restriction of service, and reciprocally, the servicemen activated the house and the Edes' keen sociality.

The attention Ede lavished on his soldier visitors is in direct contrast to the notice he took of the local people who worked at Whitestone and helped to facilitate these experiments in social composition. Mohammed al Rifi, and a man only documented as Achmet, worked at Whitestone during the Ede's time in Tangier. The log records Mohammed as helping with the house and bringing supplies; in the photographs of the Tangier period that remain in the Kettle's Yard archive, his name has been attributed to images of a man (or men) wearing jabador or djellba, garments associated with the Islamic faith and common to Morocco. In one photo he appears at a threshold, looking into the room beyond which seems to be the subject of the photographer's gaze. Elsewhere, his figure is caught walking down a steep path, or amid a posed photograph in front of the car, his facial features smeared as he looks away. In the historical record, this figure – if it is a single figure – is on the periphery, decidedly not central to Ede's social composition.

In *Ordinary Notes* Christina Sharpe remarks: 'There's no short or easy answer to the question: "Who gets to tell the story of the African Diaspora?" Likewise, there is no short or easy way to assuage the anxieties about telling a story right. Any attempt to address either must attend to power.' She states: 'who writes, how one writes – as in from what subject position – and *what* one writes matters'.[26] This is an important point about perspective, recognition and awareness, which applies to visual art too. As Himid has said: 'That is what I'm trying to paint – that crucial political everyday crashing into the personal'.[27]

In the new series of paintings *How Can I Help You?* (2025), Himid shifts perspective. Each of the five paintings includes two men – a merchant and a customer – interacting at the threshold of a shop. She has said that these scenes could be taking place on the shopping streets of Tangier, elaborating the undetailed activity that provided the backdrop for Ede's log. The men negotiate one another, some touching, some keeping a wary distance. Some are posed in their finest attire; others are apron-draped or in looser garments to facilitate a day's work; one wears a form-fitting ensemble to reveal a finely shaped figure. The drama of each encounter is framed by an open door which variously seems to pull the action inward or repel it outward.

Himid has written scripts to accompany each painting that explicate the figures' interactions but also heighten the tension by revealing the disconnect between what is said and what is thought.[28] For instance, in *Their Elegance Will Astonish You* the shopkeeper extols the exquisite taste of their potential customer, tempting him with coffee, biscuits and the finest products, while the customer thinks:

> I don't need persuading in this way, I would buy even more than I do from you already but sometimes you talk too much when all I want to do is look at everything you have on the shelves and in the storeroom.

The script goes on to reveal the shopkeeper's uncertainty – 'I wish I knew whether you really like the things I have on offer' – before the scene dissolves with the bitterness of missed understanding as the customer leaves. The script animates the figures' gestures: the customer glances sideways with lips sealed and arms crossed, his slightly bent knee seems about to be drawn into a step over the shopkeeper's feet, as the other man strides wide attempting to stop the customer's forward motion, while planting a beseeching touch on the customer's shoulder and upper arm. On the right, thin tongues of painted pattern scarves are tantalisingly draped over shelves, mimicking the shopkeeper's attempts at temptation, even though all the customer wants is to step inside and see the things kept safe in the storeroom.

In *Your Charm Offensive*, the relations are reversed. The customer reaches round the shopkeeper's shoulders, body close and eyes meeting in a steely gaze, while his other hand reveals a certain tension with an outstretched pointing figure ready to be raised in demand or threat. The script reveals the shopkeeper to be exasperated by the liberties taken by this proto-influencer, with his transparent face hiding nothing:

> Yes, I know it truly does look impressive to everyone who knows you or catches a glimpse of you walking away with armfuls of my goods. Yes, it's true it does seem to attract more customers but never enough to balance the books. I keep wondering what on earth I can do to get this relationship back on an even keel but nothing I seem to do or say to you is making any difference.

In *Repair Jobs*, the dynamic of shopkeeper and customer shifts, as the two men negotiate the dynamics of paid work and the reproductive labour of care in hospitality. Here the merchant brings a bottle out to the seated figure who is still wearing an apron. In the script he offers his company and the prospect of future work in exchange for 'wine and food'. In this painting, the floor of the entrance is an even grey that succumbs to broad strokes of orange, green and pink as if revealing layers of flooring past: a clear sign of well-trodden hospitality, enhanced by a hand reaching out from behind a curtain. Despite the warmth of the shopkeeper's welcome — both spoken and thought — he meets only an ambiguous acceptance. Arms crossed and looking wearily to the side, the customer thinks:

> Yes, I am tired and unhappy but need to look angry, especially in front of you.
> I desperately need company, a spot of wine and small amounts of food tenderly offered but am so exhausted from doing paid work, all over the city, that this offer is going to be almost impossible to take up. I wonder whether I can explain this without crying.

In this painting, and throughout this body of work, the positions and relationships between shopkeeper and customer are shown to be complex. Far from any superficial image of retail service — which may be cursory or presume a hierarchy between purchaser and seller — the figures negotiate expertise, wealth, time, confidence, feeling and desire. We get a sense of differences in class that are brokered and sometimes overturned by commodity desire, or mutual negotiations of care. There are also attempts at trust, as well as differences in opinion which both hold fast and divide. These are common experiences, ordinary dramas we all navigate. In *How Can I Help You?*, retail is an ambivalent device through which we can see these brief encounters reflected, elaborating the importance of even minor acquaintances in building a fairer, and freer world.

This ordinariness is about relatability. With their life-sized figures, these paintings seem to be of our world; they invite our identification. And yet this is not a direct invitation. The figures are tangled up in their own encounters, oblivious to us passing by or stopping to stare. Himid has said that when you enter the gallery where these works are installed, you are entering the figures' space, and we each have to negotiate our presence in relation to them. The gallery becomes a theatre of social relations. As Lisa Merrill writes: 'In Himid's exhibitions, we find ourselves simultaneously in the story she stages for us and in our own lives.'[29]

There is a politics to this ordinary relatability that resides in not knowing. On the one hand, it speaks to the gaps in archives and documents (such as the Tangier Log) that absent certain lives — often racialised, but also queer and gendered — from the record or reduce them to empirical data. There are perhaps echoes of this depersonalisation in the labelling of each painted interlocutor as 'A', 'B', 'C' etc. And yet this may also be seen another way: as a technique of 'opacity', or the work of withholding as a means of protection from surveillance or hypervisibility, which has its own long history of deathly violence.[30] Making visual art within this zero-sum scenario demands finesse well beyond the appeal to more representation. The painted figures in How Can I Help You? are not portraits, not named persons, but people living with others. While it is important that they are Black men — that they are present in the paintings, in the galleries where the paintings are installed, and more broadly in the history of art — the point is that they are quotidian, which is not to say, that they are the same as each other, or any viewer. As Himid has said: 'We are not different because of the colour of our skin. We are different because of our experiences of life.'[31]

Gilmore would argue that those 'experiences of life' are different because of the racialised social systems we live within, in which whiteness is often both the ordinary and exemplary. It is only by addressing how we relate to one another, attempting to break down existing structures that depend on the interlacing of familiarity, family, property and security, that change can happen. As Gilmore writes: 'capitalism demands inequality and racism enshrines it'.[32] Resistance to these conditions has to be both total and intimate. In Gilmore's words:

> Instead of imagining the persistent reiteration of static relations, it might be more powerful to analyse relationship dynamics that extend beyond the obvious conceptual or spatial boundaries, and then decide what a particular form, old or new, is made of, by trying to make it into something else. This — making something into something else — is what negation is. To do so is to wonder about a form's present, future-shaping design — something we can discern from the evidence of its constitutive patterns, without being beguiled or distracted by social ancestors we perceive, reasonably or emotionally, in the form's features.[33]

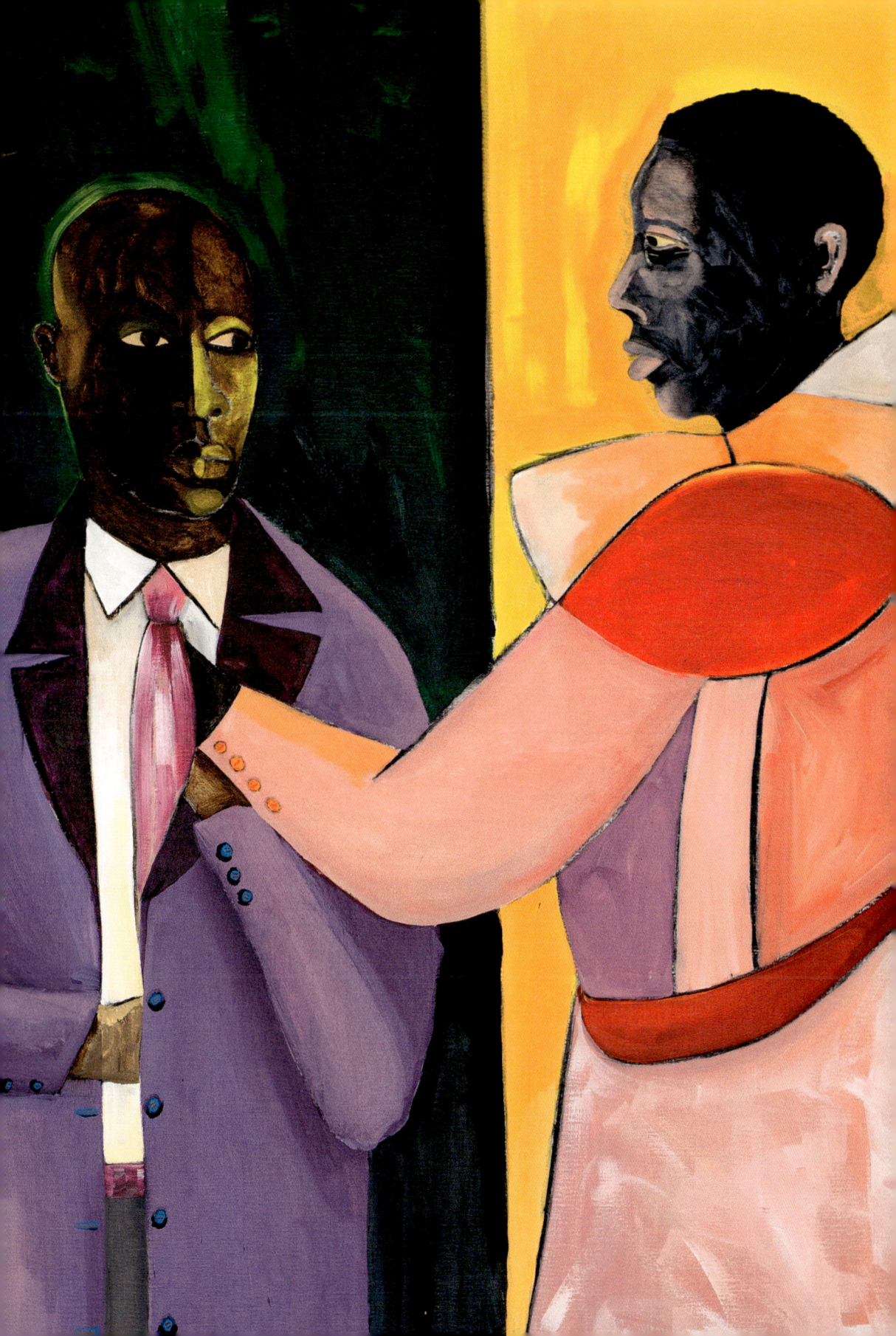

If this can take place in our lives, organisations and societies then it must also be present in art, which not only represents new forms, but by altering our orientation, comportment, or simply, attention to the world and to others, can make something into something else.[34] This is what Himid's compositional paintings do, not proscriptively with their own obscure morality of good and bad actions, but through the presentation of conscious choice.

As Himid has said:

> It doesn't matter actually who you are, but you do have to decide who you are in relation to these people whose room you have chosen to inhabit. The experience should be similar to entering a room and deciding what you're going to do, how you will react and interact. The paintings are changing every time you step through the door into them, because you were experiencing them differently to the friend who came to the exhibition with you, because your two lives are not the same.[35]

The invitation to 'rearticulate our own connections in new (and frightening) forward-looking moves' is there even in the title of this new body of work: 'how can I help you?'[36]

*

In *Favours for Years to Come,* two figures stand close together. One framed by the threshold and the bright yellow background of the space beyond, transgresses the door and the body of the other figure, sliding his hand underneath his customer's shirt. The customer's hand seems to meet it, while his other palm slides under the jacket, which from the script, we learn, he is trying on for size. The two sets of eyes meet; their feet point toward each other.

The customer thinks:

> I like the way you feel you can reach inside my shirt without really asking simply because the clothes are yours until they are mine.

While the shopkeeper thinks:

> You are a very quiet man. I like that and very beautiful too but perhaps too shy.

Until the customer asks:

> Would you like to come out to dinner with me sometime soon?

Whether or not this invitation sparks from romance and friendship, this painting stages the possibility of the retail encounter unfolding into a new composition of people, places and things. But Himid's couplings of men here, and elsewhere women, is also suggestive of myriad forms of affection, attraction and devotion that bring people together, alongside, against and in excess of the legal binds of heteronormative marriage and family. While her paintings of women represent a lifelong commitment to 'understand the women I know, how to work out complicated futures together, how to love them properly, how to take care of them, how to have myself taken care of', the paintings of men are 'strangely easier', not so subject to centuries of fixing gendered representations into certain forms of permissible or troubling femininity.[37] Nonetheless, the paintings of men resist the static postures of masculinity, showing 'men doing something that two men are never, or not usually doing in a painting'.[38] Sometimes this unusual content is shopping, comradely exchange, planning, or caring for one another; at other times, there is unmistakeable desire.

For Jim Ede, relationships with other men (and women) outside his marriage, were a constant source of nourishment. The hospitality they provided at Whitestone, and later at Kettle's Yard were preceded by bohemian dinner parties at the couple's first home in Hampstead, and mirrored in another form, in the Edes' correspondence. As I've suggested, Ede was not only interested in composing spaces and things: people were an important component in the worlds he made. In his unpublished autobiography *Between Two Memories*, Ede reflects — via a third-person narration — on this lifelong investment in others:

> Jim considered that he had never been 'unfaithful' to Helen, but that he had, in his own way, enjoyed many friendships which were entirely personal to him, which did not compete with any relationship he had with her. He seemed to have a new special friend each year [...] He used to wish he had ten hearts and it was mostly exhaustion which made him restrict himself to the few friends he did [...] When there are too many flowers to be picked a lassitude assails the picker.[39]

These friendships were characterised by Jim Ede's care and support, especially for artists:

> Jim would be lavish on a friend's behalf, spare himself nothing to obtain for them what they might need, to further their interests; all that was gratuitous, like the gifts of artists to mankind, and it is surprising how little anyone took advantage of him. He nearly always knew the pure in heart, and for these he worked. For others he worked too, but kept them at a distance.[40]

Like Jim, Helen was an avid correspondent and a great friend to artists. In *Between Two Memories*, he describes his philosophy of marriage:

Perhaps his marriage was odd in that instead of narrowing, it widened his horizon. He used to say [...] that married people should be back-to-back, so seeing all the circle of their world about them, instead of front to front, to close themselves into each other. He felt that marriage should enlarge, two people become one, to split again into a greater diversity, that diversity to spread outwards to humanity, and deriving constant support and nourishment there from.[41]

For Ede marriage, like friendship, was part of broad composition of life and he avidly pursued relationships with men based on respect, affection and sometimes desire that far exceeded the competitive bravura of normative masculinity. People were part of a lively recipe of spaces and things, and he was unsatisfied with any routine or institutionalised pattern. This was a queer sociality that both paralleled and contrasted with the bohemianism of sites such as Charleston. At Kettle's Yard, all the chairs, in their various configurations and placed in relation to so many different artworks, map the possibilities of these relations. While they remain static — part of a display that for the most part remains unchanged — the invitation to sit and enjoy the best of things, as he saw it, must now necessarily become more open and attentive to those conditions that prevent access, claim and enjoyment.

Given Jim Ede's commitment to an outward facing sociality, it is perhaps strange that one of the only literary works Ede published — and for which many know him best beyond Kettle's Yard — is his biography of the French artist Henri Gaudier-Brzeska. Published in 1931 under the title *Savage Messiah*, the book sedimented Gaudier-Brzeska's artistic reputation as a key figure of the modernist avant-garde after his early death in 1915, during World War I.[42] Ede was able to write the book because he acquired the Estate of Gaudier-Brzeska following the death of the artist's partner, the Polish writer Zofia Gaudier-Brzeska in 1925, after years of trying to secure his legacy. While numerous sculptures and drawings provided the foundation for the Kettle's Yard collection, Zofia and Henri's correspondence gave Ede great insight into his life and work. Despite Zofia's presence in these archive materials — and in Henri's work — her history and literary experiments have been diminished. Ede's focus on Henri as an exemplary figure certainly contributed to this. The social composition falls away in *Savage Messiah* in favour of a more conventional idea of the heroic, original and independent artist, despite Henri and Zofia's idiosyncratic rejection of the conventions of the time, most notable in their refusal of marriage, instead taking each other's surnames to form the portmanteau Gaudier-Brzeska.

Himid and Stawarska have sought to restore some of the complexity of this history in their collaborative installation *Slightly Bitter*. The work takes its starting point from the partial correspondence of Zofia Gaudier-Brzeska and the Welsh artist Nina Hamnett, who was a friend, model and sometime lover of Henri's.[43] Written between 1917 and 1918, while Zofia was living in parts of rural and suburban England, after her partner's early death, isolated and cut off from her familiar bohemian milieu, she reached out to Hamnett to enlist her in the effort to secure Henri's legacy, as well as to share her thoughts on literature (the poet Charles Baudelaire comes up), current affairs and everyday happenings. While only Zofia's letters to Hamnett have apparently survived, their strained relationship is nonetheless evident and compounded by Hamnett's often excoriating accounts of Gaudier-Brzeska in her autobiography *Laughing Torso*, surely animated by jealousy of Zofia's partnership with Henri, but perhaps also her xenophobia, evident elsewhere in the book blended with a noxious racism.[44]

Himid and Stawarska have worked with these texts for *Slightly Bitter*, extracting sections that appear across the numerous elements of the installation that the artists have worked on both independently and collaboratively. The title alludes to the awkward aspects of Gaudier-Brzeska and Hamnett's relationship after Henri's death, and the difficulties of betrayal and dependence. Each of them ambitious, their bitterness is also suggestive of the feeling of chagrin that can attend professional and creative disappointment, especially for women artists and writers working in hostile conditions. While sour feelings are usually the subject of gossip or anecdote rather than history, here Himid and Stawarska acknowledge them as an honest response to an unequal world. Given that the artists have also merged their personal correspondence — alongside other meaningful fragments of their lives — with those of Gaudier-Brzeska and Hamnett, they also lay a claim to this bitterness, marking the stresses and strains of their own careers and intimate relationships. Seen in contrast to the encounters staged in *How Can I Help You?* — which depict more compassionate relationships between men — *Slightly Bitter* may allow for a little more acrimony to be acknowledged, without shame, between women.

Throughout the installation, bitterness also appears in the form of lemons and limes. Lemons are a frequent and versatile motif in

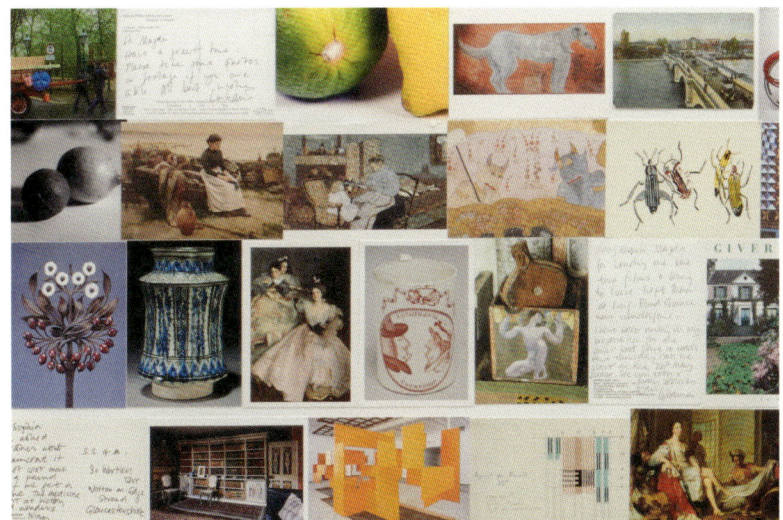

Magda Stawarska and Lubaina Himid, *Slightly Bitter* (detail), 2025

Himid's work, where they take on mercurial meanings — sour, savoury or saccharine, fresh or cloying — but they are also important to Kettle's Yard and the Edes' compositions of space. In the Kettle's Yard cottages, famously, a lemon sits on a pewter plate where it creates a visual harmony with the yellow ellipsis of Joan Miró's *Tic Tic* (1927) hanging nearby, a favourite illustrative example of Jim Ede's. Meanwhile the coupled lemon and limes in *Slightly Bitter* pick up on the title of Stawarska's soundwork for the house, *The Sharp Sweet Taste of Limes*, a line from Lorde's *On a Night of the Full Moon* in which the poet addresses her lover, comparing her body's taste to the juice of the lime. This erotic imagery reminds us of the powerful alchemy of sweet and sour, pleasure and pain that characterises desire, and structures romantic love. In this intimacy, as well as in the richness of their decades-long collaboration that reaches a crescendo in *Slightly Bitter*, Himid and Stawarska diverge from the brief almost-friendship of Zofia Gaudier-Brzeska and Nina Hamnett.

These two relationships, nonetheless run like parallel tracks in *Slightly Bitter*. For instance, Stawarska's long piece of printed and painted paper, yellow with a series of blue strokes, is reminiscent of a watery conduit with a series of postcards floating on its surface. These cards, some face-up, illustrate important places to the Gaudier-Brzeskas around Putney and Fulham in South London (where they lived and worked after leaving France) and face-down annotated with notes between Himid and Stawarska, recording Stawarska's opportune encounter with Gaudier-Brzeska's studio along one of her regular London running routes. While this channel stops midway along one gallery wall, a thin band of printed zinc encircles the space entirely. It is annotated with lines from Gaudier-Brzeska's letters to Hamnett, which implore her to visit. Some of these phrases repeat audibly in the space, along with other fragments from the letters and Hamnett's prose. Voices resonate in Polish, French and English, accents change the intonation of certain words, and at points the speakers attempt to teach one another the trickier phonemes of their

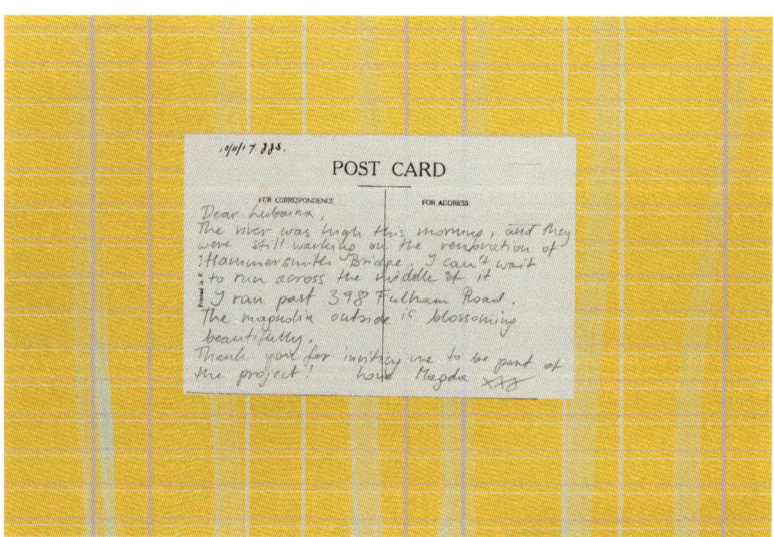

Magda Stawarska and Lubaina Himid, *Slightly Bitter* (detail), 2025

respective languages. On the far wall of the gallery, the phrases 'slightly bitter' and in Polish 'nieco gorzko' are spelt out phonetically, as if to invite the reader to join in the chorus of voices. Aside from revealing another dimension of Gaudier-Brzeska and Hamnett's encounter, these works shape our attention, drawing us into the noise and complexity of life.

The combination of English, Polish and French emphasises the multi-linguistic experience of many migrants who negotiate belonging through familiar and less familiar tongues. Gaudier-Brzeska's writing moved between those three languages and in her letters, she signs her name with different stylisations – Zofie, S.S.G.B., Zophia, Zofia – betraying the shifts in identity we make as we speak and write, which is only heightened when moving across languages. This is an experience that Stawarska identifies with as a native Polish speaker who has lived and worked in England since the 1990s, which she has dramatised in the sound element of *Slightly Bitter* through the contrast between Himid's received pronunciation and her accented English.

Slightly Bitter, then, includes both a literal conversation between Stawarska and Himid, as well as representing the exchanges the two artists have long shared 'about what is seen, what is heard, what is remembered, and what is imagined'.[45] Stawarska's juxtapositions of diverse, precise yet dysfunctional grids as the backdrop for many of the elements in *Slightly Bitter*, are also suggestive of their shared project of trying to shift established patterns and conventions. As Stawarska asked of an earlier collaboration *Blue Grid Test* (2020), 'How to visualise and then offer the freedom to invent patterns?', and in reply: 'Present an open grid upon which anything can be transcribed'.[46]

In *Slightly Bitter*, Stawarska gives us these open grids, which shift and collide in irregularity like systems without alignment or perfected order. This, in turn, connects to (and in this exhibition sometimes directly collides with) Himid's passion for patterns, and especially the recurring motif of the wet-on-wet grid – in which lines criss-cross, appearing to stream colours in a single stroke of multiple pigments. There is an invitation here to speculate on what can be known, and what can be done when the pattern is not a rigid form to fit within, but a matrix for blending and colliding seemingly distinct histories, interests and commitments. Across these works, Himid and Stawarska bring patterns together in every imaginable configuration. In this they invite us to try out some new ways of relating to take the irregular, the difficult and the discordant with the harmonious, and try once again to relate, to transform, to liberate. This is a political necessity. As Gilmore has demanded: we need a 'radical dependency': 'there is so much doing involved in making ourselves free'.[47]

1   Lubaina Himid, letter of application to Kettle's Yard Artist in Residence Scheme 1997–1998, Collection of Lubaina Himid, Preston, consulted December 2024.

2   Lubaina Himid, 'Beach House', *Beach House*, Wrexham: Wrexham Library Arts Centre, 1995, p.12

3   Lubaina Himid interviewed with Magda Stawarska by Amy Tobin, 24 April 2025.

4   Himid, untitled notes toward application to Kettle's Yard Artist in Residence Scheme 1997–1998, Collection of Lubaina Himid, Preston, consulted December 2024.

5   Himid, letter of application to Kettle's Yard Artist in Residence Scheme.

6   Ruth Wilson Gilmore in Azzurra Crispino, 'The Case for Prison Abolition: Ruth Wilson Gilmore on COVID-19, Racial Capitalism & Decarceration', *Democracy Now*, 5 May 2020. https:// www.democracynow. org/2020/5/5/ ruth_wilson_gilmore_ abolition_coronavirus

7   Brenna Bhandar and Alberto Toscano, 'Editor's Introduction: Report from Occupied Territory', in Ruth Wilson Gilmore, *Abolition Geography: Essays on Liberation*, London, Verso, 2022, p. 2 and Ruth Wilson Gilmore, 'Where Life is Precious, life is Precious', *On Being with Krista Tippett*, 30 March 2023. https:// onbeing.org/programs/ ruth-wilson-gilmore- where-life-is-precious- life-is-precious/

8   Gilmore, 'Where Life is Precious, life is Precious'.

9   Ruth Wilson Gilmore, 'In the Shadow of the Shadow State', *Abolition Geography: Essays on Liberation*, London, Verso, 2022, pp. 224–241 (240).

10 Gilmore, 'Where Life is Precious, life is Precious'.

11 Ruth Wilson Gilmore, *Change Everything: Racial Capitalism and the Case for Abolition*, London: Verso, 2024.

12 This question appears on the kanga painting *How Do You Spell Change?*, 2018.

13 See 'Composing with Paint and Sound: Christine Eyene in conversation with Lubaina Himid and Magda Stawarska-Beavan', *Lubaina Himid*, edited by Michael Wellan, London: Tate, 2021, pp. 118–127 (118).

14 Lubaina Himid, 'Zanzibar', artist's statement, https:// lubainahimid.com/ portfolio/zanzibar/.

15 Dorothy Price, 'A Sense of Place: Lubaina Himid and the Sea', Wilhemina Barns-Graham Trust Annual Lecture 2025, British Academy London, 20 May 2025. Over the last two years *Zanzibar* has formed the centrepiece of two collaborative exhibitions by Himid and Stawarska: *Deep Water, Plaited Time*, Sharjar Art Foundation (2023–2024) and *Nets for Night and Day* at Mudam Luxembourg Luxembourg – Musée d'Art Moderne Grand-Duc Jean (2025), both curated by

Omar Kholief. It also appeared in *Rewinding Internationalism: Scenes from the 1990s, today*, Van Abbemuseum, Eindhoven, Netherlands in 2022.

16 Lubaina Himid in 'On the Pleasures of Opera: Griselda Pollock in conversation with Lubaina Himid', *Lubaina Himid*, edited by Michael Wellan, London: Tate, 2021, pp. 16–28 (22).

17 Omar Kholief, *Magda Stawarska*, Berlin: Sternberg Press, 2024, p. 82.

18 Stawarska quoted in Lubaina Himid, 'Afterword: Listening', *Magda Stawarska*, Berlin: Sternberg Press, 2024, p. 122.

19 Lubaina Himid, 'Some Thoughts from the Artist on Clothes and Patterns', *Lubaina Himid*, edited by Michael Wellan, London: Tate, 2021, pp. 70–73.

20 Audre Lorde, 'On a Night of the Fall Moon', *Cables to Rage*, 1970. Republished in Audre Lorde, *Collected Poems*, New York: W. W. Norton & Sons, 2000, p. 53.

21 Lubaina Himid in conversation with the author, 7 July 2025.

22 The Edes left Tangier in 1940 during the war when the city was occupied by Spanish forces. They returned in 1945. See also Andrew Nairne and Eliza Spindel, 'Tangier Days', June 2020, https://www. kettlesyard.cam.ac.uk/ stories/tangier-days- part-one/.

23 H.S. Jim Ede, 'Variations on a Weekend Theme' or 'Tangier Log', Kettle's Yard archive, np (p. 1).

24 Ede, 'Variations on a Weekend Theme', np (p.1).

25 Ede, 'Variations on a Weekend Theme'.

26 Christina Sharpe, *Ordinary Notes*, Toronto: Alfred A. Knopf, Canada, 2023, p. 71.

27 Himid in 'On the Pleasures of Opera', p. 26.

28 These scripts are reproduced on pages 48–57 of this book.

29 Lisa Merrill, 'The Exhibit as Theatre', *Lubaina Himid*, edited by Michael Wellan, London: Tate, 2021, pp. 104–110 (109).

30 On 'the right to opacity', see Èdouard Glissant, *The Poetics of Relation*, Ann Arbor, MI: University of Michigan Press, 2000 [1997], especially 'For Opacity', pp. 189–194.

31 Himid in 'On the Pleasures of Opera', pp. 24–26.

32 Ruth Wilson Gilmore, 'The Worrying State of the Anti-Prison Movement', *Abolition Geography: Essays on Liberation*, London, Verso, 2022, pp. 449–453, (451).

33 Gilmore quoted in Bhandar and Toscano, 'Editor's Introduction: Report from Occupied Territory', p. 9.

34 The relationship between art and abolition is present in some of Himid's earliest works, most obviously in the juxtaposition of George Jackson's *Soledad Brother* with Cheikh Anta Diop's, *The African Origin of Civilisation: Myth or Reality* in *A Fashionable Marriage* (1986).

35 Himid in 'On the Pleasures of Opera', p. 24.

36 Gilmore quoted in Bhandar and Toscano, 'Editor's Introduction: Report from Occupied Territory', p. 19.

37 Himid in 'On the Pleasures of Opera', p. 22.

38 Himid in 'On the Pleasures of Opera', p. 22.

39 H.S. Jim Ede, *Between Two Memories*, unpublished manuscript, Kettle's Yard Archive, pp. 53–54.

40 Ede, *Between Two Memories*, p. 54.

41 Ede, *Between Two Memories*, p. 71.

42 H.S. Ede, *Savage Messiah: A Biography of the Sculptor Henri Gaudier-Brzeska,* Cambridge and Leeds: Kettle's Yard and Henry Moore Institute, 2011 [1931].

43 Only Zofia Gaudier-Brzeska's letters have survived. They were published in English in Sophie Brzeska, *Matka and Other Writings*, London: Mercury Press, 2008.

44 Nina Hamnett, *Laughing Toso*, London: Virago Press, 1984.

45 Magda Stawarska, 'Airmail Letter: Notes on a *Blue Grid* Test', *Water Has a Perfect Memory,* London: Hollybush Gardens, 2022, p.27.

46 Stawarska, 'Airmail Letter', p. 27.

47 Gilmore, 'Where Life is Precious, life is Precious'.

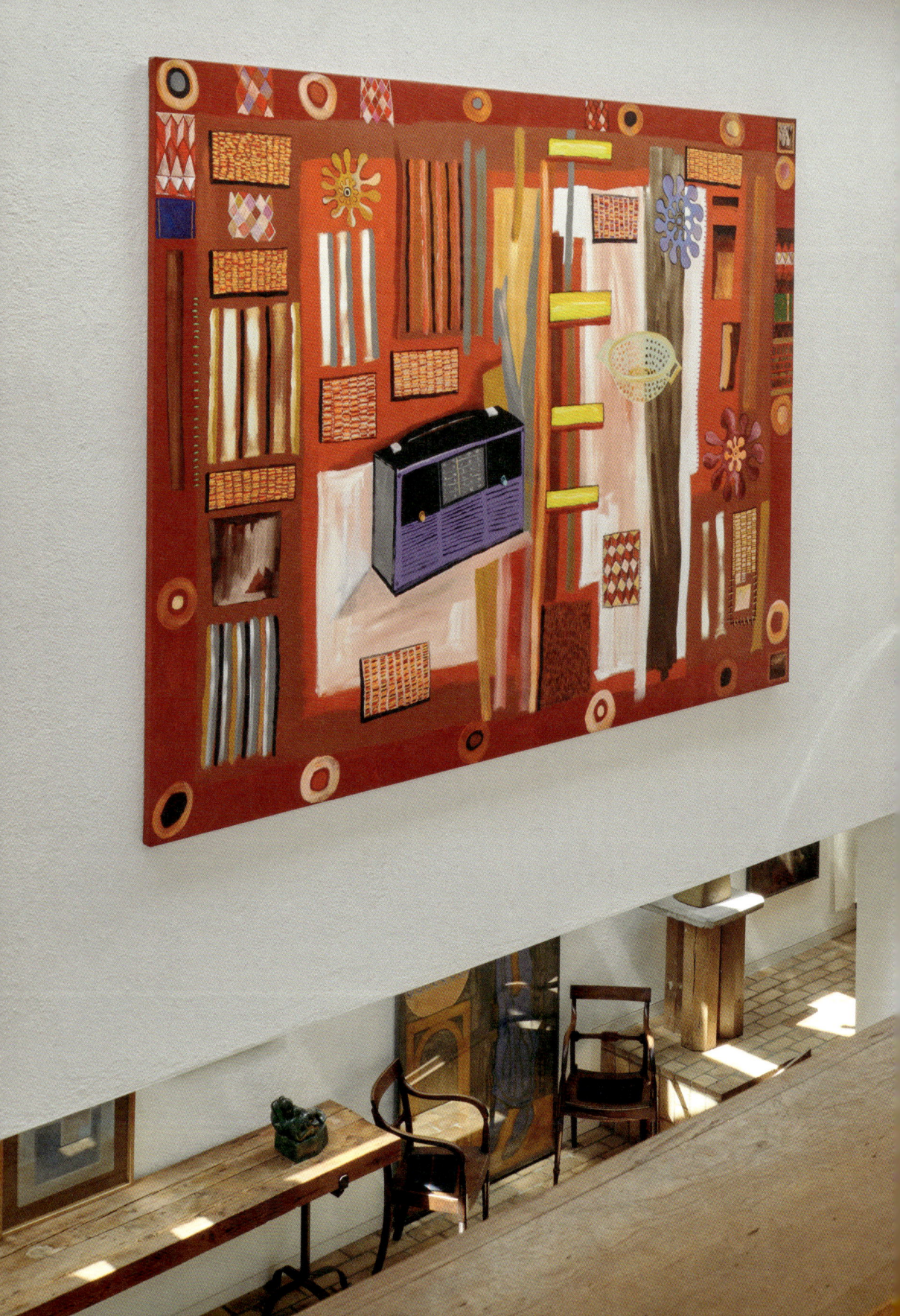

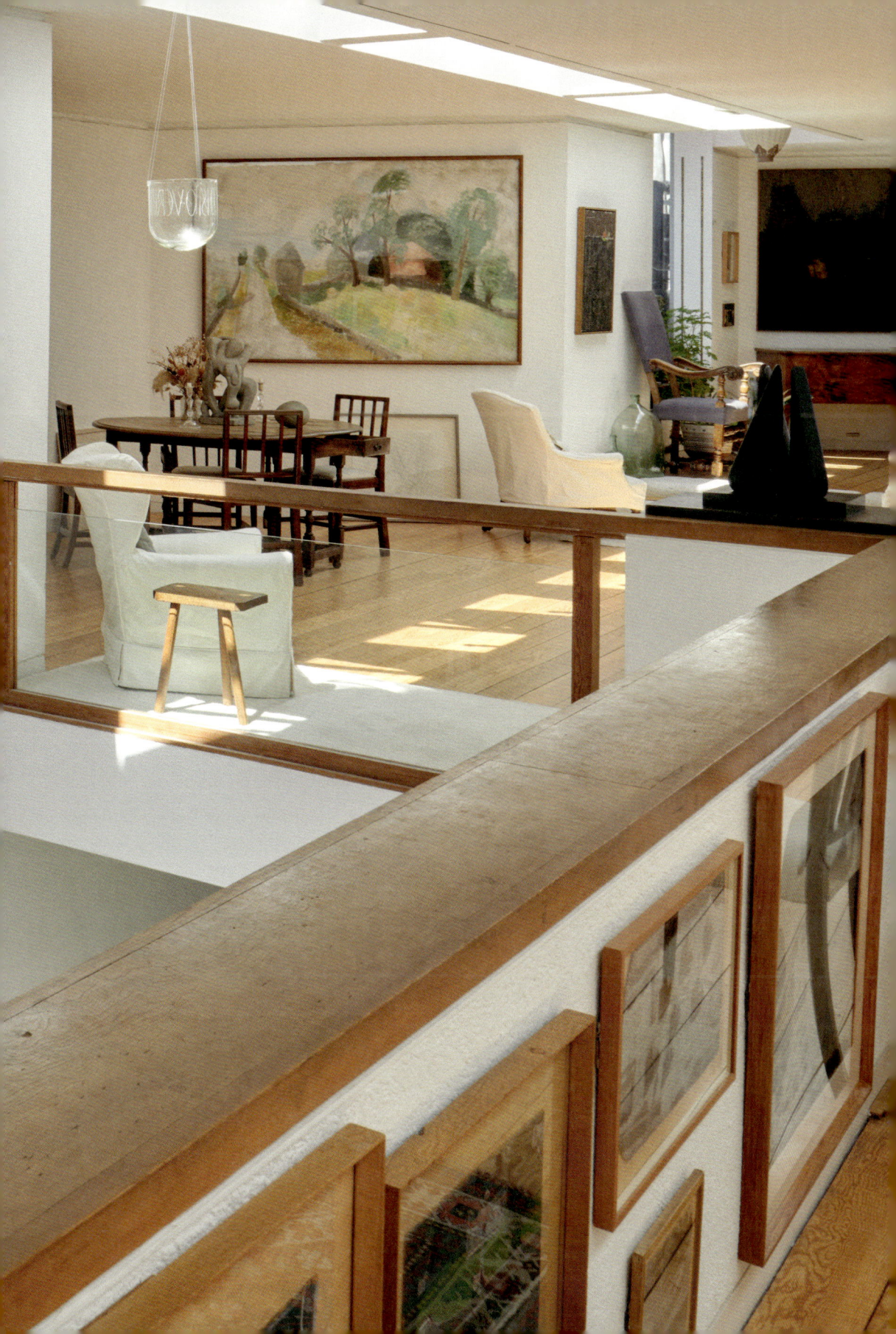

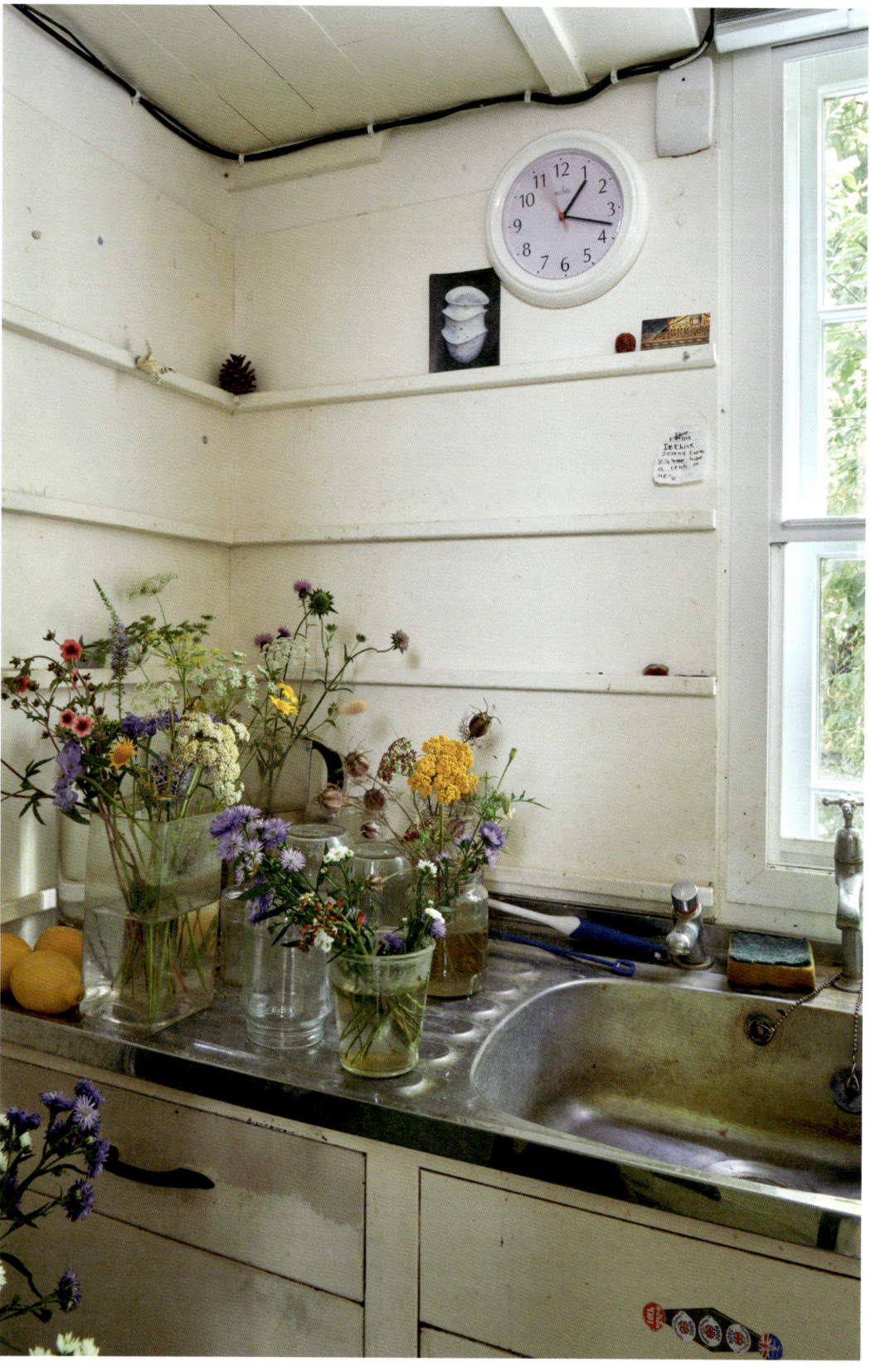

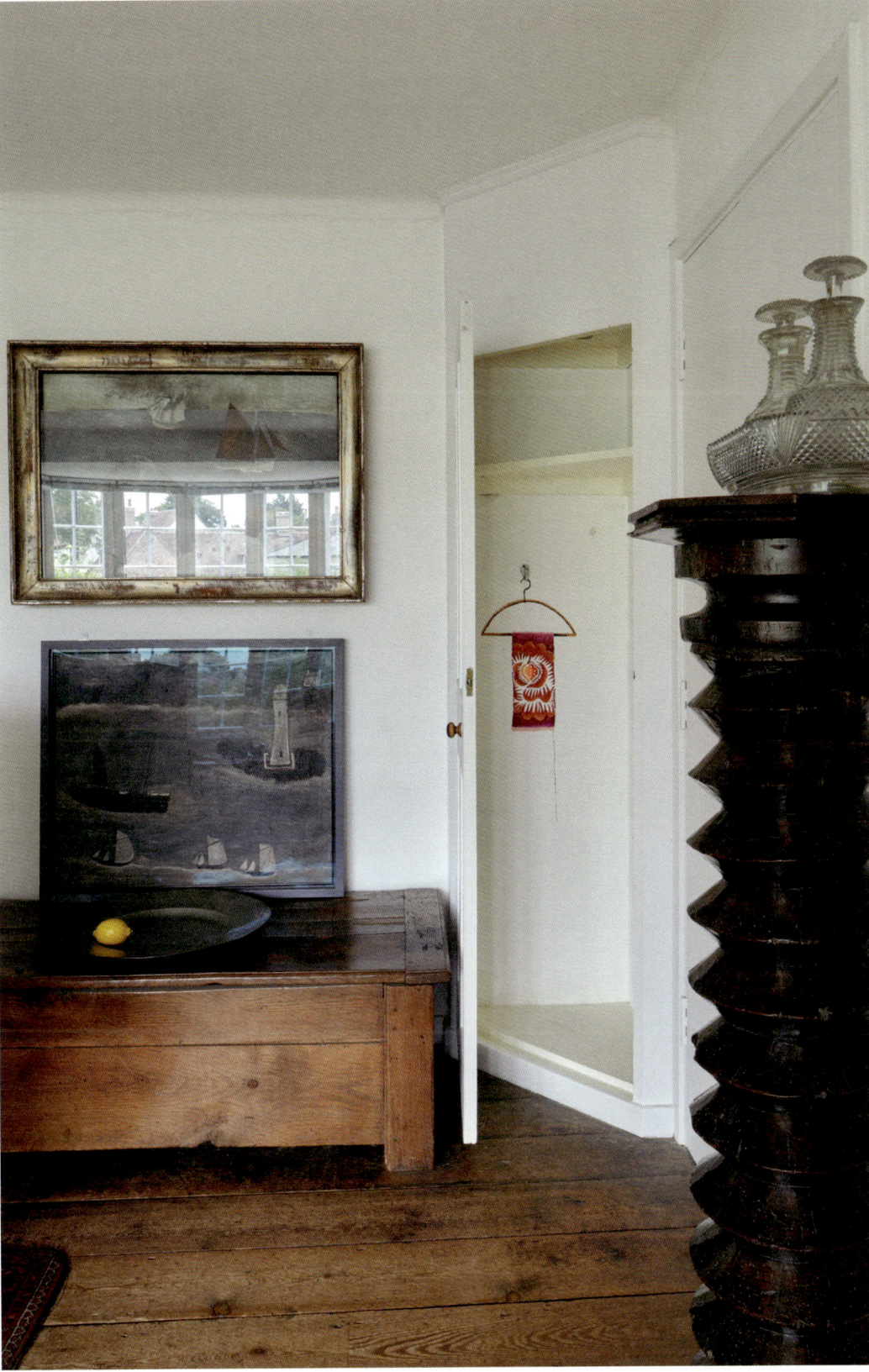

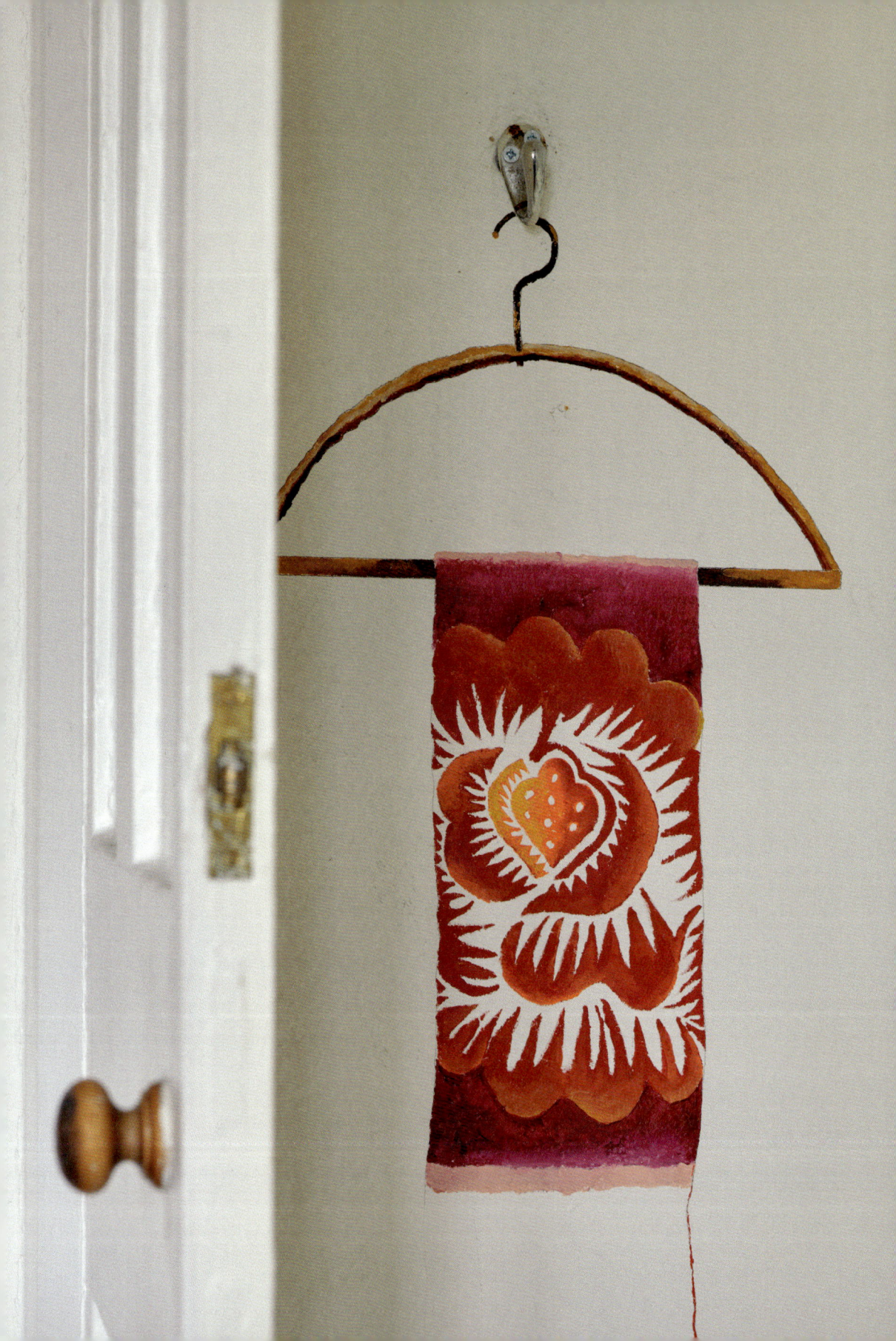

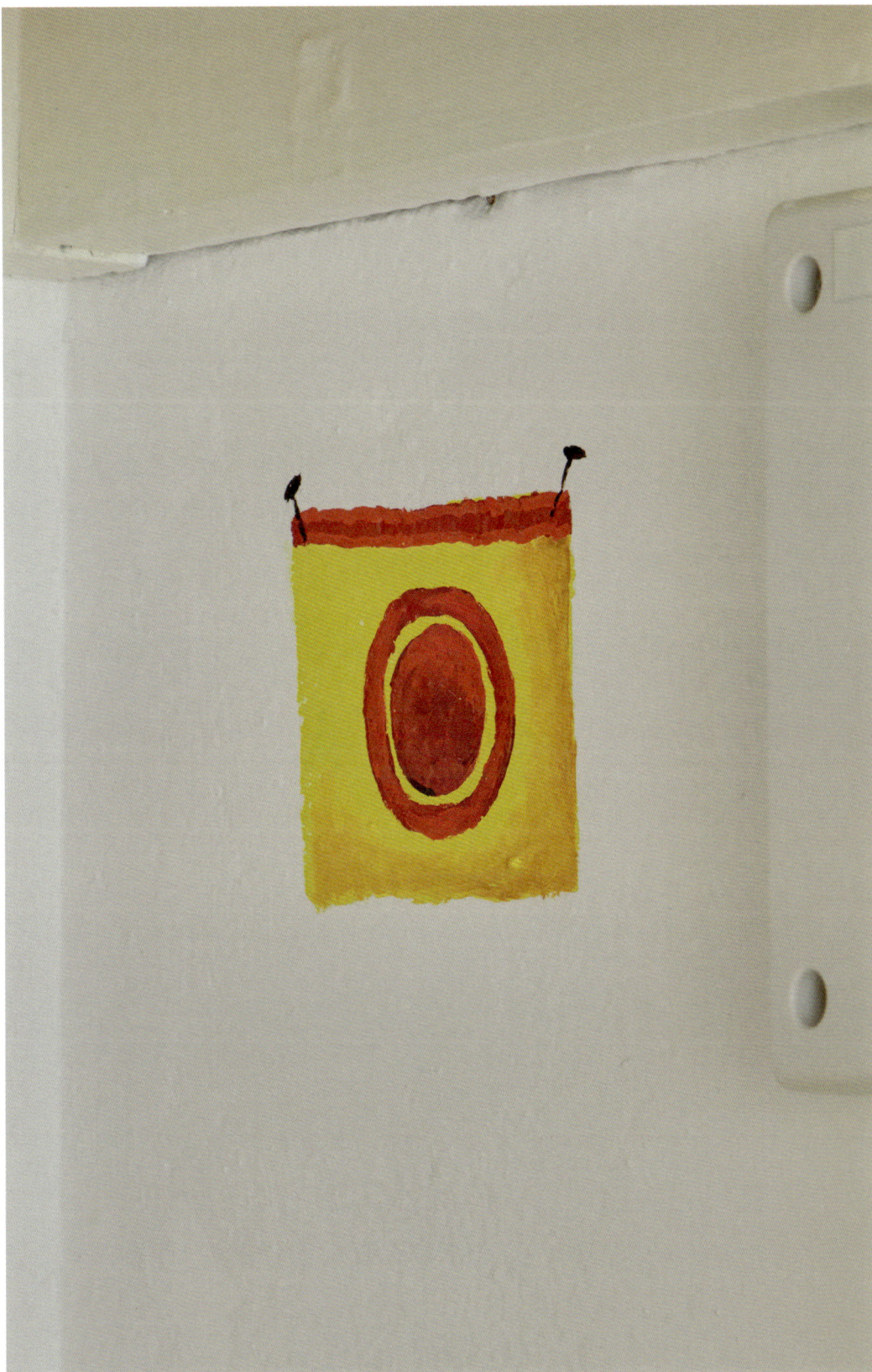

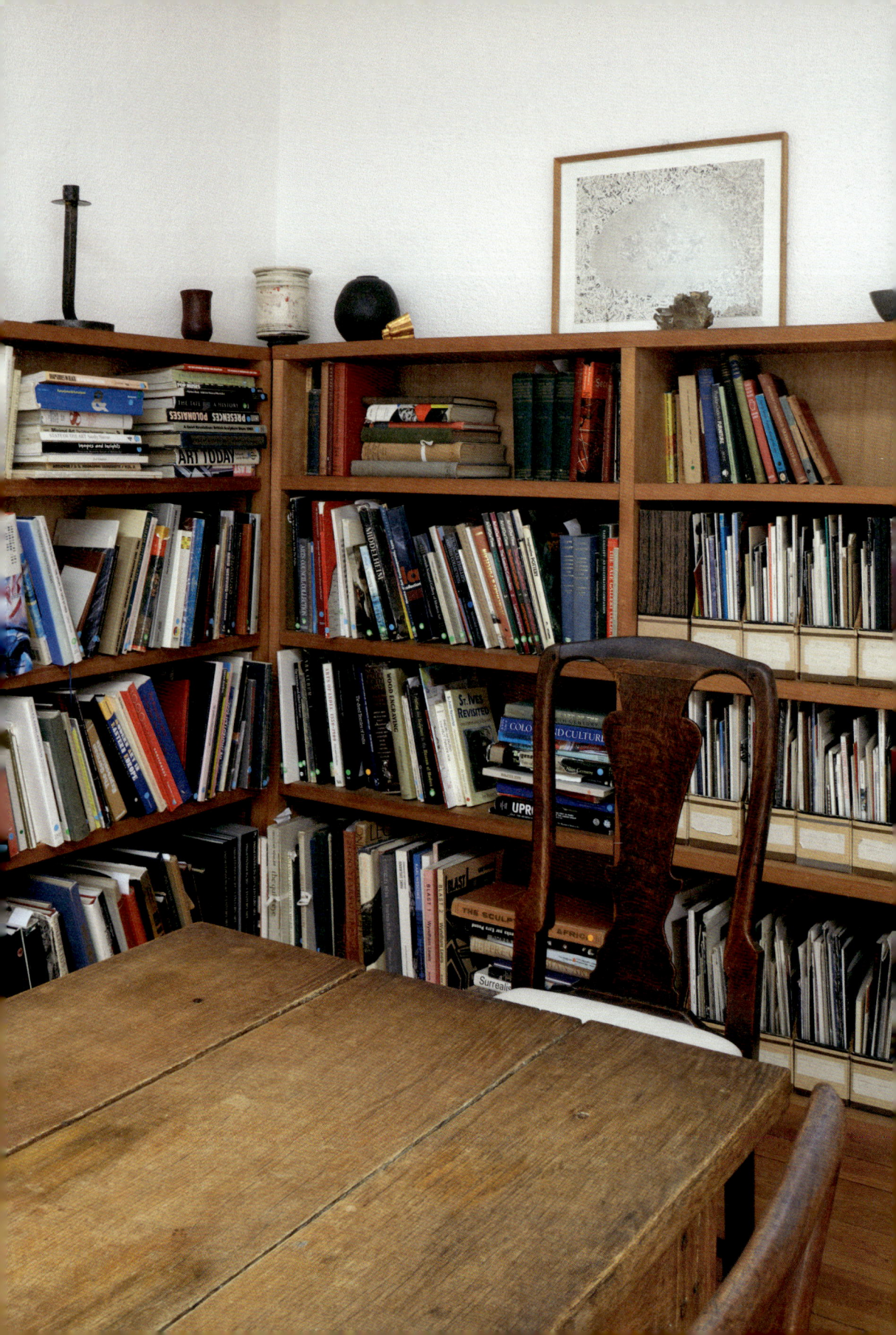

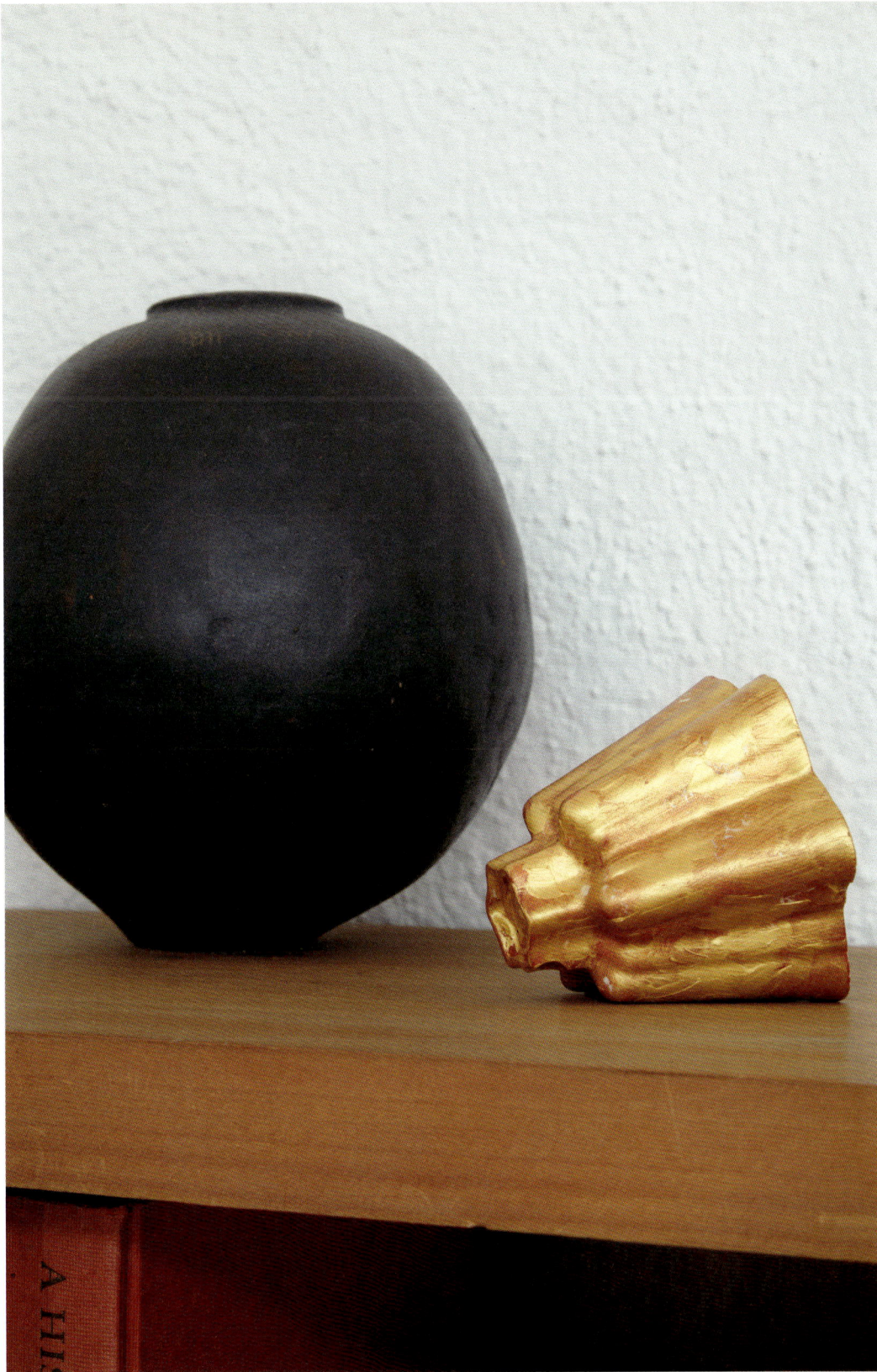

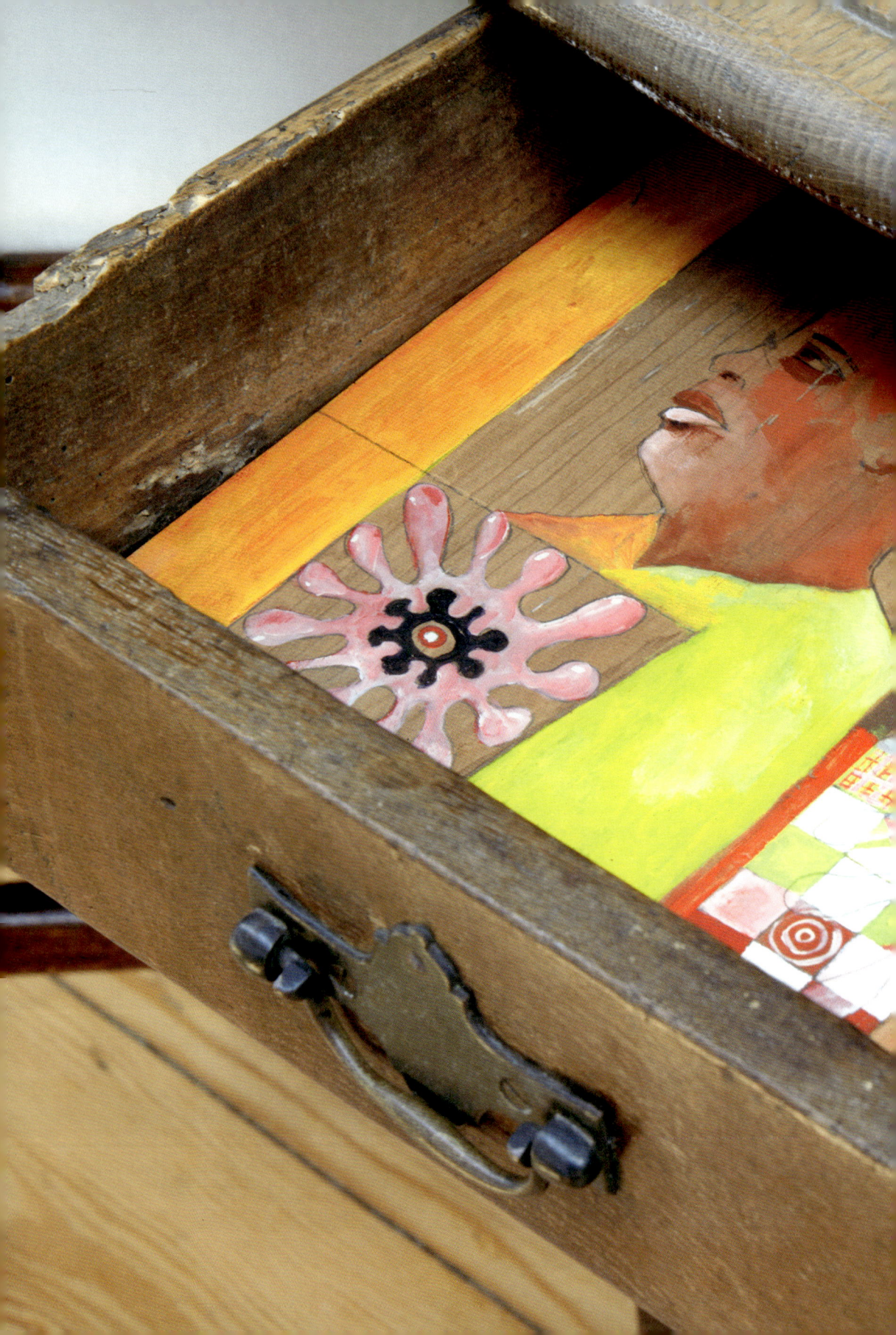

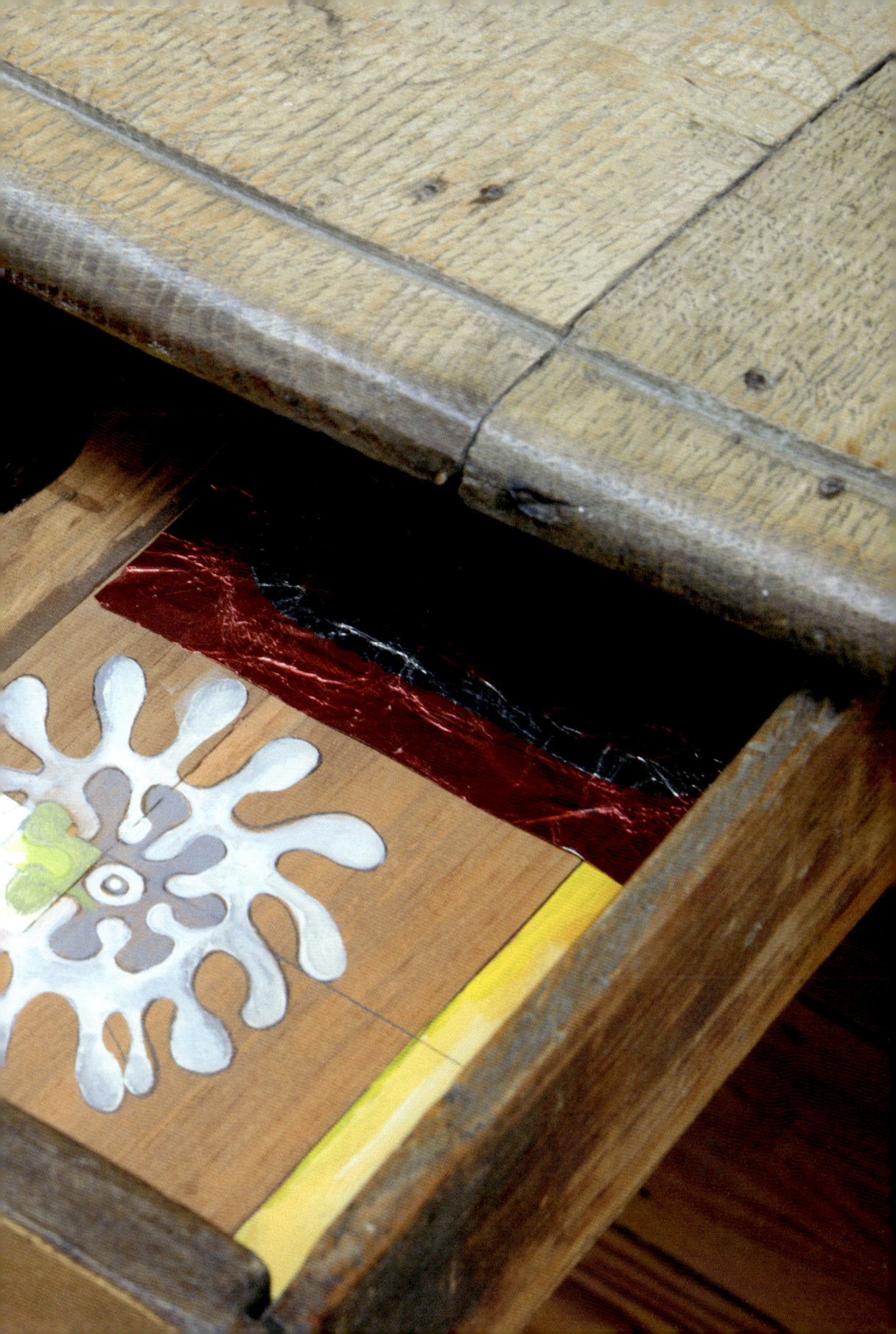

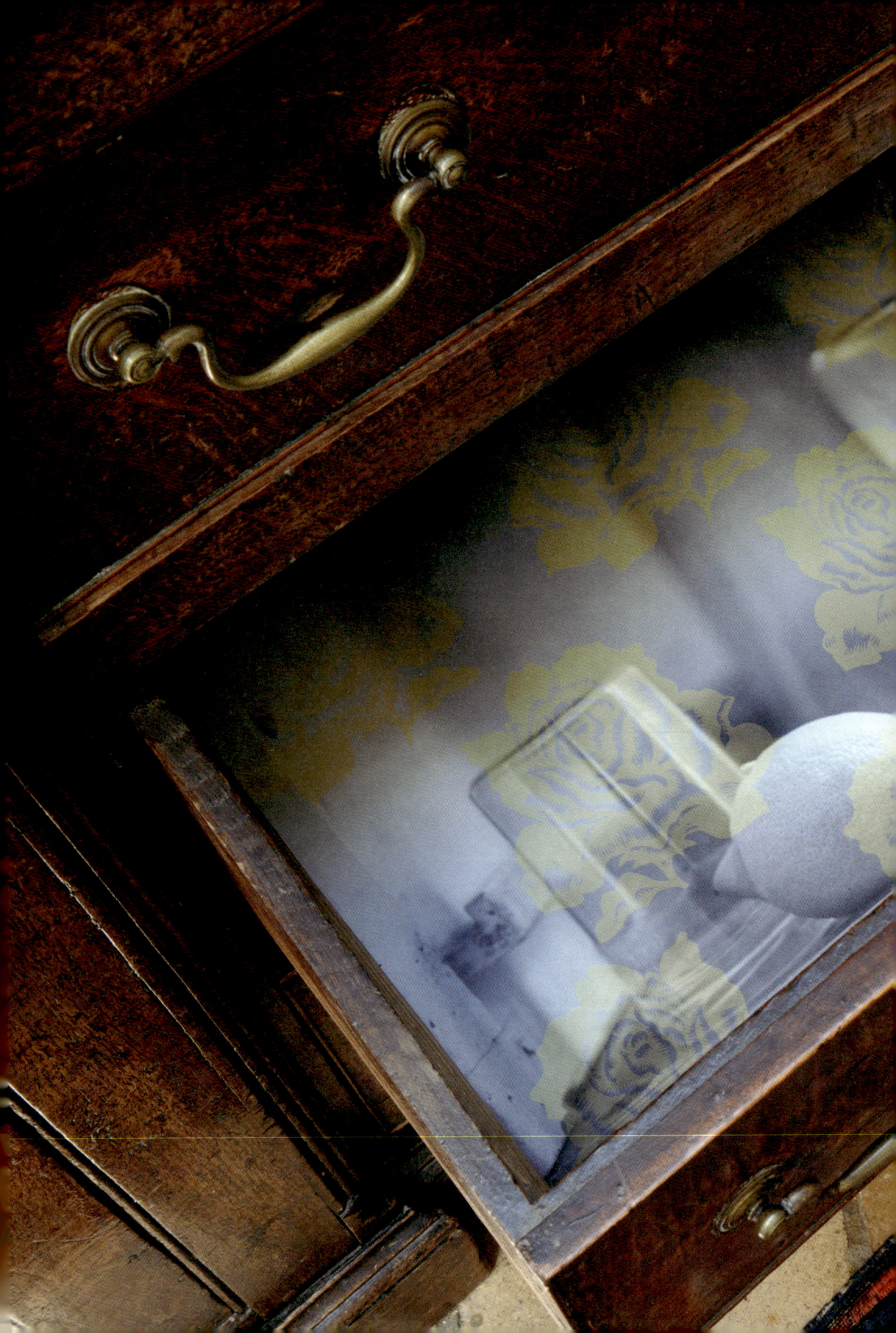

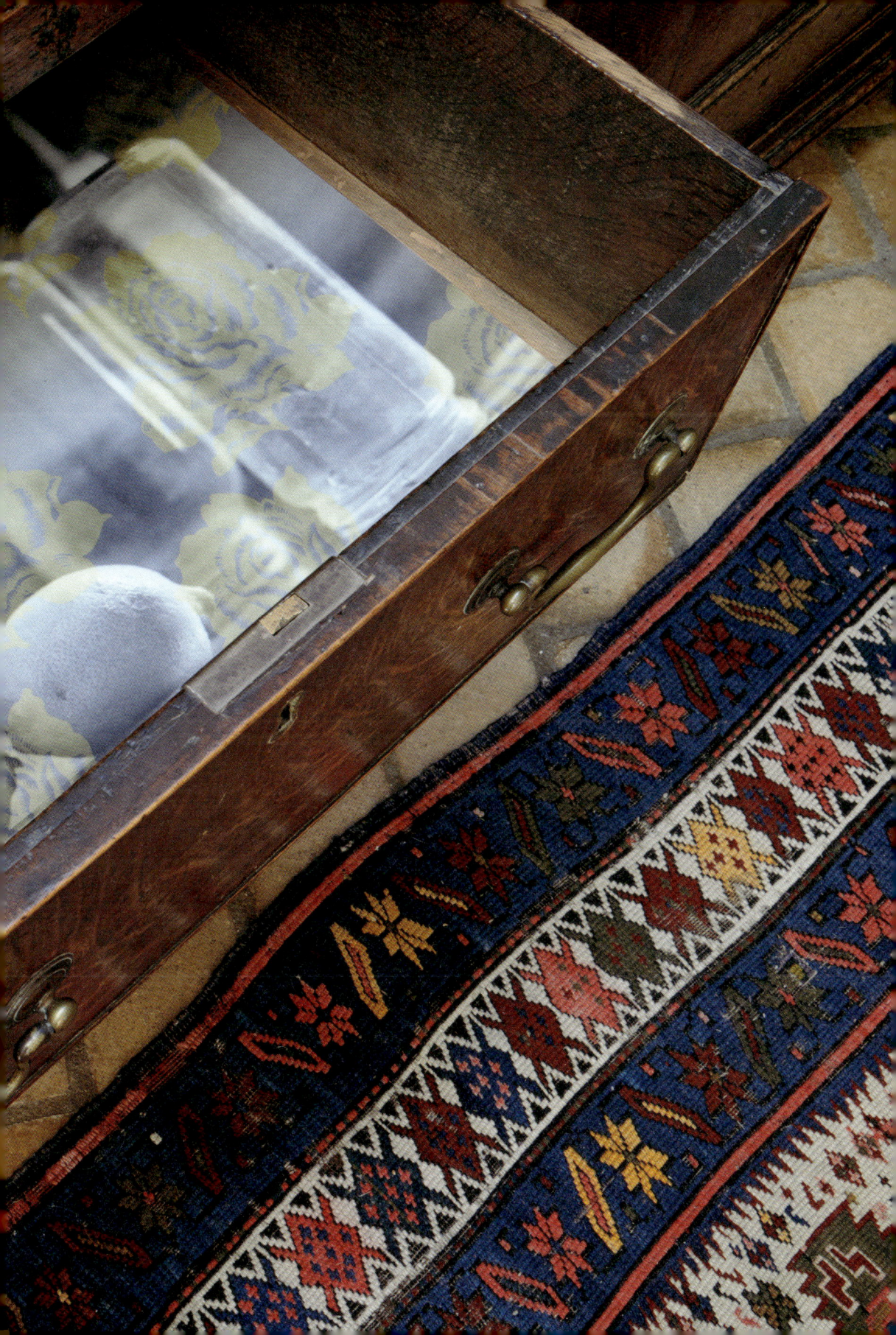

Amelia Groom

'Time is a continuous spiralling thing, rather than a long, convenient, straight thing,' Lubaina Himid tells me, via video call from her studio in Preston. She continues:

> Someone might have the same feet as their great-grandfather, and if that's true, then it's probably also true that there are all sorts of other things moving around and through us, which are also traces of the past — like the things you know when you don't know how or why you know them. I'm always dealing with this, and it's part of Magda [Stawarska]'s work too, when she's looking at cities and listening for the resonances of what's left in a place, and what has disappeared from it. For both of us, there is always this movement of circling back and going in and out and around, and opening things up and looking behind and underneath things (sometimes literally).[1]

For their collaborative exhibition *Another Chance Encounter*, Himid and Stawarska have applied these modes of spiralling back — and looking behind and under — to Kettle's Yard and certain marginalised aspects of its history. Kettle's Yard was founded by the British curator and collector Jim Ede and his wife Helen Ede. He was the author of *Savage Messiah* (1931), a popular biography of the French sculptor Henri Gaudier-Brzeska, which was made into a film by Ken Russell in 1972. Ede was able to write that book because he had acquired the estate of Zofia Gaudier-Brzeska, a Polish writer who was Gaudier-Brzeska's partner. They met in Paris and moved together to London. He added her last name to his. He ended up dying, at the age of 23, in the World War I trenches. She was left distraught and died a decade later in an asylum. Her estate included his estate, so Ede ended up with all of it. His biography of Gaudier-Brzeska draws from Zofia's letters, while largely writing her out of the picture.

Separately (from very different angles) and together (through their own entanglements as artistic collaborators and partners), Himid and Stawarska became interested in Zofia Gaudier-Brzeska and her relationship with another woman, Nina Hamnett, a Welsh artist and writer who went to Paris in 1914 and, later in life, became known as the Queen of Bohemia because she was good at partying and promiscuity.

Back in London, Hamnett posed for Gaudier-Brzeska, who made a series of sculptures of her nude torso. She wrote a memoir and called it *Laughing Torso* (1932). Himid recalls that she first read *Laughing Torso* thirty years ago, when she was interested in the presence of Black artists in Paris in the early twentieth century, and looking for any traces that might have made it into Hamnett's frame, however peripherally. Later,

Himid learned that Hamnett and Gaudier-Brzeska had written letters to each other. And Stawarska, who was interested in what it was like to live as an immigrant in early twentieth-century Britain, had read and written about the Polish translation of Gaudier-Brzeska's posthumously published, unfinished autobiography, *Matka*.

So Himid had her own relationship with Hamnett, and Stawarska had a particular relationship with Gaudier-Brzeska, and then it turned out that Hamnett and Gaudier-Brzeska had been part of each other's lives, through their chance encounter via Henri. Meanwhile, through what started as another chance encounter, Himid and Stawarska found themselves increasingly a part of each other's lives. In Himid's words, 'Here we are, two women who have had totally different backgrounds. I came to this country from Zanzibar as a baby. Magda came from Poland as a 20-year-old. Both of us ended up in this strange, quite boring northern town, working at the same university, and then making work together, and then, eventually, being together, though that took more than twenty years.'

All these relations and intimacies became the raw material for the exhibition *Another Chance Encounter*, which weaves various threads of connection, disconnection, exchange, translation, and conversation (both recorded and imagined) between and across these four women – two of them in the present; two in the past.

The new multimedia installation *Slightly Bitter* draws from the letters Gaudier-Brzeska wrote to Hamnett. The installation also engages with the histories of Gaudier-Brzeska and Hamnett's lives in relation to Henri Gaudier-Brzeska and Jim Ede and Kettle's Yard. But, Himid, is quick to point out, 'It's not a documentary; there's a lot of making it up, and a lot of building a tiny idea into a much bigger idea.' Woven through the installation are a number of postcards that were ostensibly written by Brzeska and Hamnett, but were actually written by Himid and Stawarska. Himid also painted a series of what she calls 'Fake Nina Hamnetts,' imagining and recreating long-lost paintings or possible paintings that are mentioned in *Laughing Torso*, for which no known documentation exists. Himid continues:

> We are not scholars on Zofia and Nina. We don't have a new theory; we haven't written a PhD on their relationship. We were more interested in taking their chance encounter and playing with it and building on it. That's what artists should be doing; it's not about making a documentary, it's about transmitting what we know, and getting people to remember what they already know, and getting people to know things differently. It's the same with my solo work. If a historian comes along and says to me, "How do you know this happened? Where is your evidence for this?" I would say, "I feel it." I have read about things like captive Africans stuck on boats, I have read enough narratives and spent enough time thinking and feeling. I am not doing this as a historian saying "This is exactly what

happened, on this day, to these people, and here's the evidence."
I can't paint a documentary account, but I can paint the pain of it,
or the confusion of it, or the injustice of it, or the unresolvedness
of it, or the damage that has ensued from it. That's not about
evidence; it's about knowing enough to know that this is real.

In addition to the collaborative installation, *Another Chance Encounter*
also includes a series of new paintings by Himid. The thinking behind
them started with the fact that Jim and Helen Ede — before they moved
to Cambridge and started Kettle's Yard — had lived for some years in
Tangier. Himid's painting *Flying Carpet* (2025) refers to the Moroccan and
Algerian carpets that can be found throughout Kettle's Yard (which was
the Edes' home). 'Nobody knows very much about these carpets,' Himid
tells me, 'but they were obviously bought in those places.' Ever attuned
to the gaps and omissions that can be traced in the historical record, the
artist was first and foremost interested in what has been left out of the
story about the Edes' years in North Africa:

> The way it's been told, you get the feeling that Jim and Helen lived
> this isolated life in their beautiful, very comfortable home up on the
> hill. You hear about Jim going to pick up [Truman] Capote or Gore
> Vidal as they arrived by airplane, but you never hear about what it
> was actually like to live in Tangier. What did they eat? Where did the
> food come from? Somebody — servants, Black servants — went to
> get the food, and prepare the food, but you never hear about that.
> And you never hear about the encounters and relations within the
> life of the place.

On view in the first room of *Another Chance Encounter*, Himid's series
How Can I Help You? (2025) is an attempt to imagine some of those
unrecorded passing relations. The canvases are large; the figures life-
sized. The textures vibrate, and the colours are gorgeously bold. Each
painting in the series depicts two men conversing by a doorway, at the
threshold of a shop or other small business that could be in Tangier. Himid
has written a series of texts to accompany the scenes, imagining the
kinds of exchanges that might happen between vendors and potential
customers in such semi-public spaces.

As with the *Slightly Bitter* installation, these paintings take
selected historical or biographical details as a starting point — but only
as a starting point. Jim and Helen Ede lived in Tangier between 1936 and
1952, with a break during the years of World War II. That much is known.
But Himid's paintings come from a practice of relating to history through
attunement to the structuring forces of erasure, exclusion, and forgetting.
A practice of looking at what's missing from the narrative; studying the
shapes of the archival gaps; feeling the contours of the holes; listening
for the imposed silences; and imagining creatively at the margins of the
historical record — and at the point where the record cuts off.

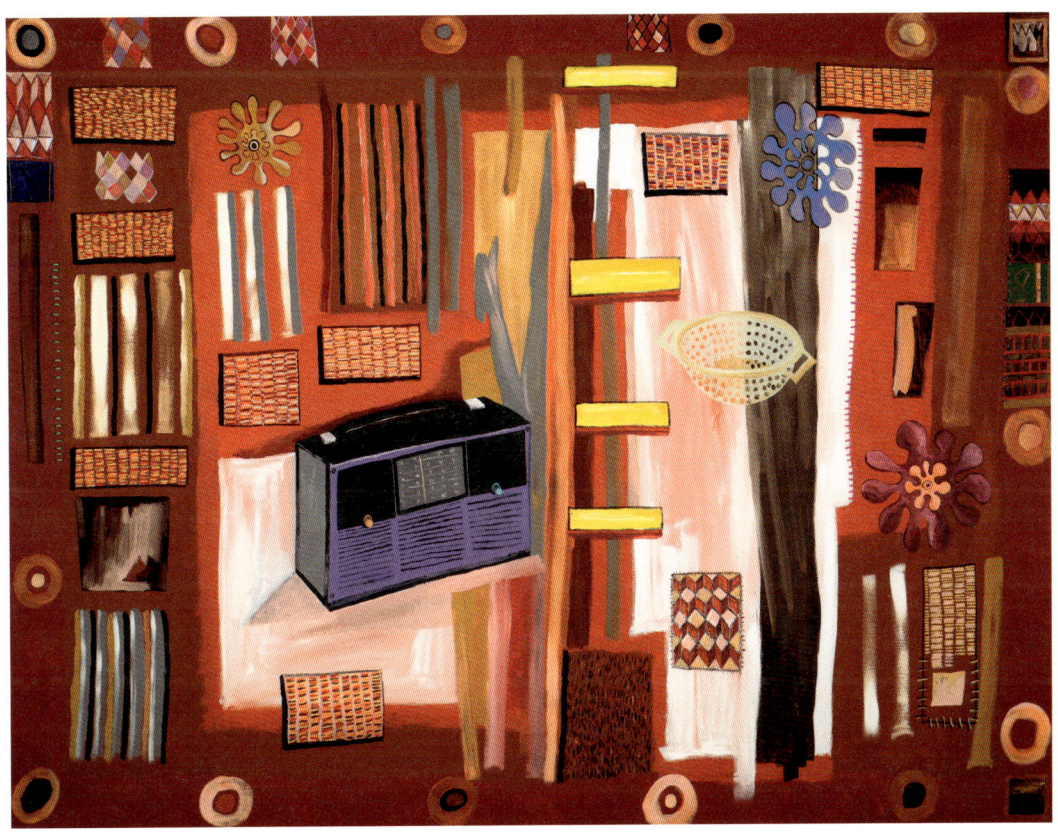

Lubaina Himid, *Flying Carpet*, 2025

This kind of approach can be traced right throughout Himid's oeuvre over the last four decades. Her early cut-out installation *A Fashionable Marriage* (1986) reworked William Hogarth's satirical painting *Marriage A-la-Mode: The Toilette* (1743), updating his eighteenth-century figures for the contemporary climate of Thatcher's 1980s. As part of this installation, Himid looked to the Black figures who appeared in the original painting in predictably peripheral and anonymised background positions. The figure of the enslaved servant who stands in the centre of Hogarth's composition while simultaneously being pushed into the background, offering a beverage to the white aristocrats who constitute the foreground, is, in Himid's hands, transformed into the figure of a Black woman artist. Close to nine feet tall, she wears an elaborate, oceanic dress and occupies a centre point in the scene. As with the *How Can I Help You?* series, the figures who have been pushed to the margins and kept out of sight within the historical record are resuscitated and brought onto Himid's stage with their own stories, specificities and agencies.

The mid-1980s were the height of what has become known as the British Black Arts Movement (after the earlier Black Arts Movement in the United States during the Civil Rights era). As a leading figure in this movement, Himid curated a series of exhibitions of young Black and Asian women artists: *Five Black Women* (The Africa Centre, 1983), *Black Woman Time Now* (Battersea Arts Centre, 1983), and *The Thin Black Line* (Institute of Contemporary Arts, 1985). During an interview for the BBC series *Desert Island Discs*, she recalls that this was a time when 'The notion of Black people being artists was completely alien to people in the British art world; people actually said to me "Black people don't make art."'[2] Facing this dearth, the challenge was not just to find a way to show her own work, but to help create a context in which her work could exist alongside the work of other Black artists.

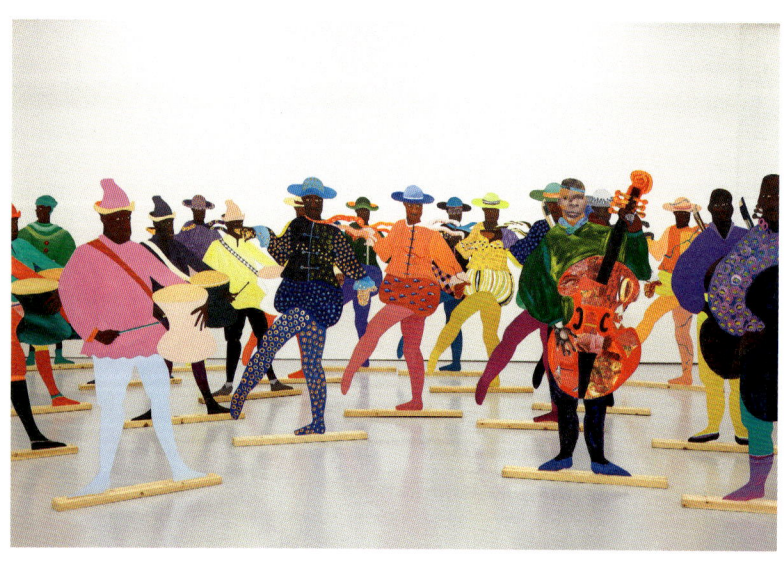

Lubaina Himid, *Naming the Money*, 2004. Installation view, 2017

Looking back on this era, Himid tells me she now finds herself less drawn to working on a large scale with direct confrontation and persuasion. 'I used to want to change the culture,' she says. 'I used to think that was possible, but Black artists just become occasional colouring-in for the existing state of things, while nothing really changed.' She continues:

> I've become interested in working on a much tinier scale, and thinking about very small encounters – very subtle, simple, everyday things. Some people have said to me, "Your work is not angry anymore, not the way it was forty years ago." My response to that is to say, "Well, I am still angry, but it's true, the work isn't shouting at you, it doesn't give you that thrill." In a lot of what I'm doing – including in this collaboration with Magda – it's not about interrupting history to try to change the culture directly. It's more about paying attention to the chance encounters and the minor details and the forgotten nobodies along the way.

I suggest to Himid that there might seem to be a shift away from working on a large, confrontational scale, but, at the same time, her work has always been committed to attending to small details and finding powerful resonance in the ostensibly minor or irrelevant.

Take, for instance, one of her most ambitious and well-known works, *Naming The Money* (2004), which comprises one hundred slightly larger than life-sized free-standing cut-out figures, accompanied by a soundtrack. Once again looking at how Black people have appeared in the history of European painting, Himid examined depictions of servants and entertainers who arrive in the pictorial frame only in positions of support and servitude for their white masters and mistresses (who are portrayed as main characters with complex interior lives and names that are remembered). *Naming The Money* turns the nearly invisibilised background of European white supremacy and ease into an exuberant foreground, with all these peripheral figures given their own stage, their own names and stories. The supporting roles become the main characters, and those forced to the margins come together in a busy, polyvocal centre. Himid's words:

> It's true; *Naming The Money* was about giving these Black people their names back and opening up to those minor details – how someone who is only seen as a servant or a maid from the outside, actually has a whole being, full of details. You have love, you have passions for things, you don't like the taste of tomatoes, whatever it is, the full dimensionality of the person, because you're not just this nameless, faceless serving thing. And it's probably just where I'm at in my life now, but I'm starting to feel that maybe that's the answer to everything. Because once you actually understand that, and you truly sense that this other person is important, really

important as a whole being – then you simply could not invade their country, you couldn't take their things, you couldn't, you know, treat them worse than you would treat yourself, because you would understand they are on exactly the same level as you.

Now in her seventies, Himid has, in the last decade, received a string of belated accolades (being elected as a Royal Academician, receiving a CBE, being chosen to represent Britain at the 2026 Venice Biennale and becoming the first Black woman to win the Turner Prize, to name just a few). One aspect of her practice that can end up pushed to the edges in a focus on her illustrious career as a solo artist is the fact that she has always wanted to have other artists on the stage with her.

In the early 1980s, she took out advertisements in *Art Monthly*, looking for other young Black artists in Britain, to send them a questionnaire about their work and experiences of exclusion within the art world (this research resulted in her 1984 thesis at the Royal College of Art, 'On Being a Young Black Artist in Britain Today: A Political Response to a Personal Experience'). Her aforementioned work as a curator also came from her early interest in and engagement with the work of other artists. When an interviewer on the podcast *Talk Art* suggested to Himid that it was generous of her to create these spaces for showing work by other artists, she was adamant that it wasn't about generosity, it was about *not wanting to be alone*. 'It isn't generosity at all,' she said, 'I never want to be the only one.'[3]

Before she became a painter, Himid had worked in theatre design in the 1970s, and she traces her ethos of collaboration back to that context. 'Working in theatre is a team thing,' she has said. 'The director might think they're in control, the designer thinks they're in control, the actors think they're in control and of course the writer thinks they're in control, but actually there's a kind of fabulous collaboration.'[4] The artist's collaborative practice with Stawarska is part of this long trajectory.

When Himid paints people, they are quite often in pairs or groups. The *How Can I Help You?* series is a recent example of her long-standing interest in showing people encountering each other, relating to each other, not wanting to be alone. To look back to another early project from the 1980s, Himid's watercolour series *Scenes from the Life of Toussaint L'Ouverture* (1987) honours the life of the most prominent leader of the Haitian Revolution. The artist recalls that she learned about L'Ouverture while avidly reading C. L. R. James's *The Black Jacobins* (1938) and Wenda Parkinson's *This Gilded African* (1978). But rather than remember him as an individual hero, *Scenes from the Life of Toussaint L'Ouverture* imagines ordinary details about his daily life, including the food he ate, his knowledge about local herbs, his love of horses, his friendships with other revolutionaries, and his relationship with his wife, who may have helped him with strategy (once again, in the absence of hard evidence, at the margins of the historical record, speculation and imagination come to the fore in particular ways). This approach, which honours the life of a prominent historical figure while situating him within his networks of relations and affinities, is grounded in a feminist ethics and aesthetics that divests from the maintenance of the myth of the isolated individual.

All of this provides a framework for some of what's going on in *Another Chance Encounter*, where the interest is in relationality rather than individuals. While Zofia Gaudier-Brzeska and Nina Hamnett have often been relegated to the footnotes or pushed off the stage entirely in the telling of stories about the lives of men like Jim Ede and Henri Gaudier-Brzeska, *Another Chance Encounter* is not an exercise in salvaging these women as overlooked geniuses who can now be erected as individual pillars. Indeed, there is nothing romanticising in the way Gaudier-Brzeska and Hamnett are encountered here. Himid describes Hamnett as 'a dreadful snob in that weird and slightly repulsive English way.'[5] In one of her letters to Hamnett, she writes,

> You always describe other people in terms of their nationality and do not bother with their names. Even one of your numerous lovers you describe as "my Pole", other men you describe as "the abominable Pole" or "the extremely nice Pole" or "the other Pole". Unsurprisingly, you describe a stocking seller as an "Old Jew" and two artists models as "a large Negro and his wife". You talk about Russians, Spaniards, South Americans, the Arab or without saying anything real or personal about them. You describe the hair of the daughter of the President of Liberia as funny, short and woolly. It's painful for me to read.

Gaudier-Brzeska comes off as more endearing, but Himid and Stawarska are not interested in treating anyone in isolation here. Instead, they explore modes of storytelling that are nonlinear and inconclusive, allowing for complex relations that criss-cross through the historical record, and extend beyond it with added layers and unearthed traces and speculative leaps.

1   All quotations, unless stated otherwise, come from the author's interview with Lubaina Himid, 11 June 2025.

2   Lubaina Himid, *Desert Island Discs*, Sunday 2 June 2019, https://www.bbc.co.uk/programmes/m0005mfp.

3   Robert Diament and Russell Tovey with Lubaina Himid, *Talk Art,* podcast episode, Thursday February 11 2021 https://shows.acast.com/talkart/episodes/lubainahimid

4   Cited in 'Composing with Paint and Sound: Christine Eyene in conversation with Lubaina Himid and Magda Stawarska-Beavan' in *Lubaina Himid*, edited by Michael Wellen, London: Tate publishing, 2021, pp. 118–121 (118).

5   See Luabina Himid, 'Letter to Nina Hamnett', in this volume, p. 86.

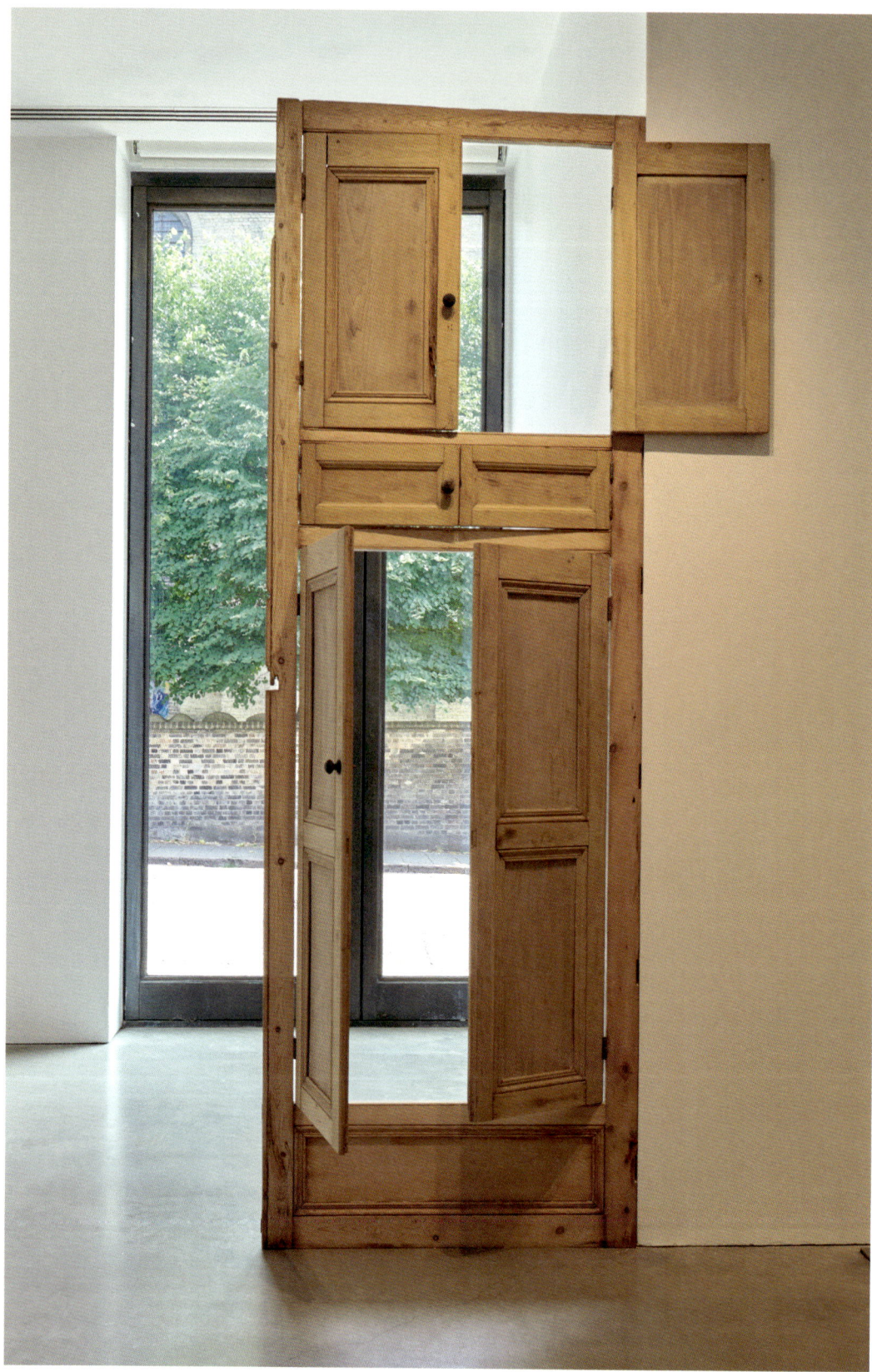

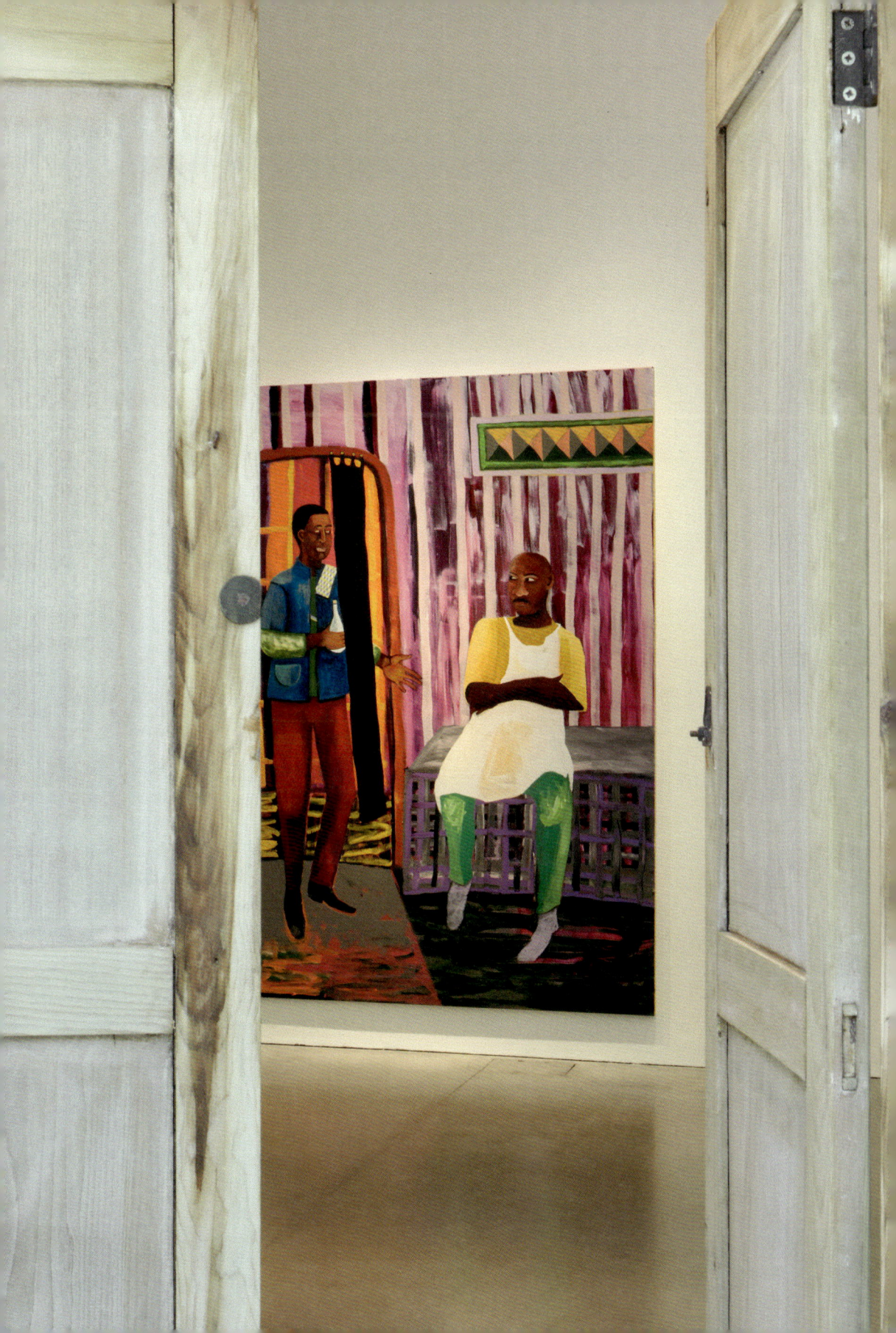

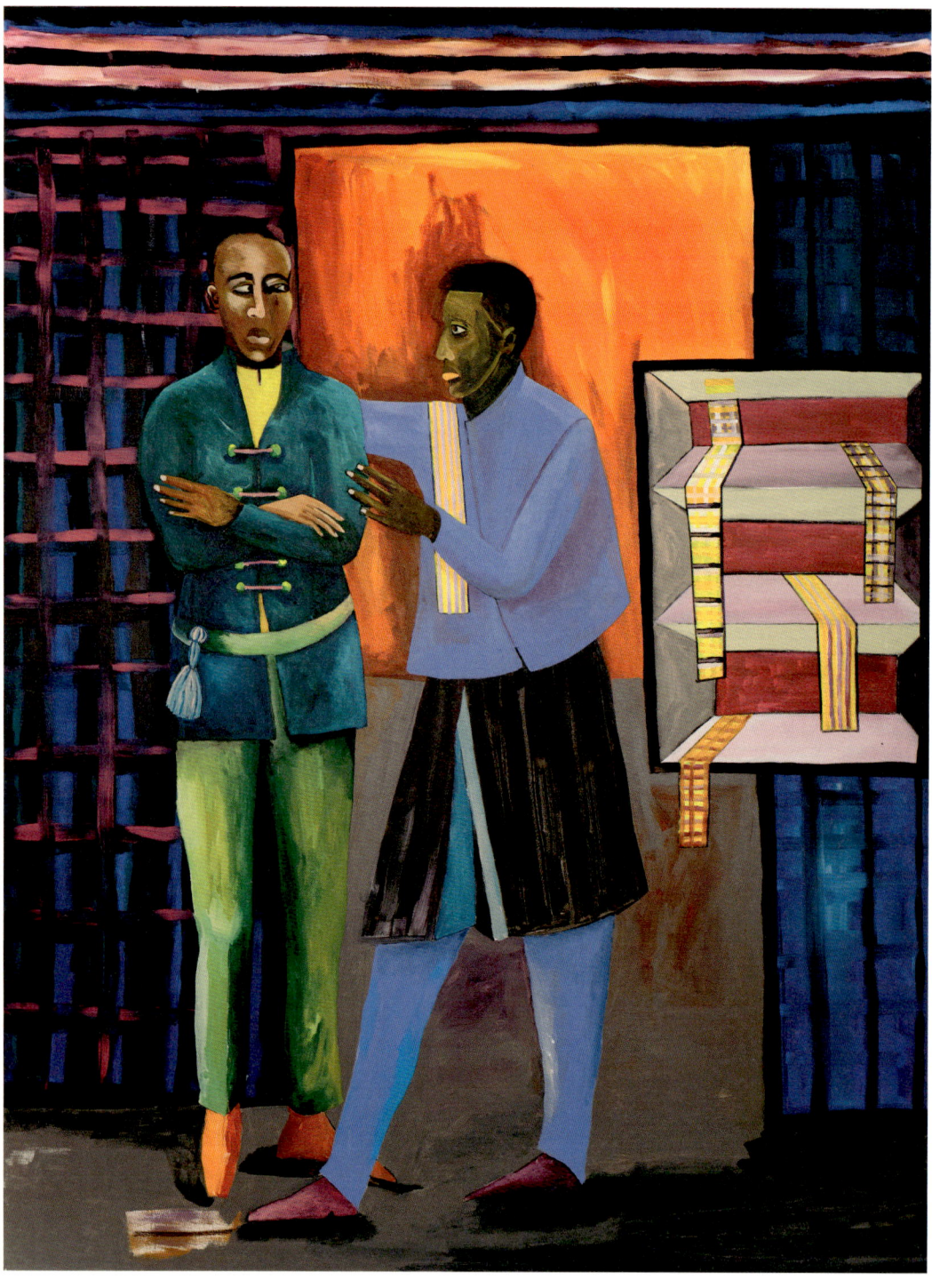

Lubaina Himid, *Their Elegance Will Astonish You*,
from the series *How Can I Help You?*, 2025

Lubaina Himid

1
Their Elegance Will Astonish You

A. Speaking

I'm so happy you came to my little shop today I have some beautiful examples to show you.

It's so good to see you again, have you been away or just busy with your new company? These beauties I have here were only delivered to me at the beginning of the week and I haven't shown them to anyone else. As soon as I opened the parcel, I absolutely knew that you would love them, their elegance will astonish you. The quality is quite special and the price is remarkably reasonable. If you have time, please stop here a while and have a cup of my best coffee and I'll show you everything I have. If you are short of time today, at least look at one or two examples to whet your appetite. There are so few men who understand what happens when exquisite pattern and gorgeous fabric meet, so it is always such a pleasure to work with you.

B. Thinking

I don't even need persuading in this way, I would buy even more goods than I do from you already but sometimes you talk too much when all I want to do is look at everything you have on the shelves and in the storeroom, drink a few cups of your wonderful coffee and eat one or two of those delicious biscuits you make, then spend my money and leave until the next visit in a months' time. Please calm down and let me stay a while with you, in silence, simply looking and feeling the quality of the weave.

A. Thinking

I wish I knew whether you really like the things I have on offer and whether you will ever have time to come into the store room and look at some of the most special pieces I am reluctant to sell because I love them so much.

B. Speaking

I must go now, I have several important meetings to attend.

C. Speaking

Here my friend, allow me help you sort that. The shirt almost fits but could do with some tiny alterations, don't worry, your body is perfect by the way.

Yes, the design of the coat is supposed to look awkward. I agree it's not meant to feel awkward! The colour suits you; we chose well and the fabric really will do you a lot of favours for years to come. I hope you are happy with the buttons, as you know they are my speciality. I chose them with you in mind, knowing that you love them to be small and numerous — twelve is the ideal number for this coat.

D. Thinking

I like the way you feel you can reach inside my shirt without really asking simply because the clothes are yours until they are mine. Your hands are always warm but never sweaty or unpleasantly clumsy. Ha, I like the casual compliment you slipped in as you seemed to be fussing over fit and feel. I love the way you make me look and this helps the way I feel.

C. Thinking

You are a very quiet man. I like that and very beautiful too but perhaps too shy.

D. Speaking

Would you like to come out to dinner with me sometime soon?

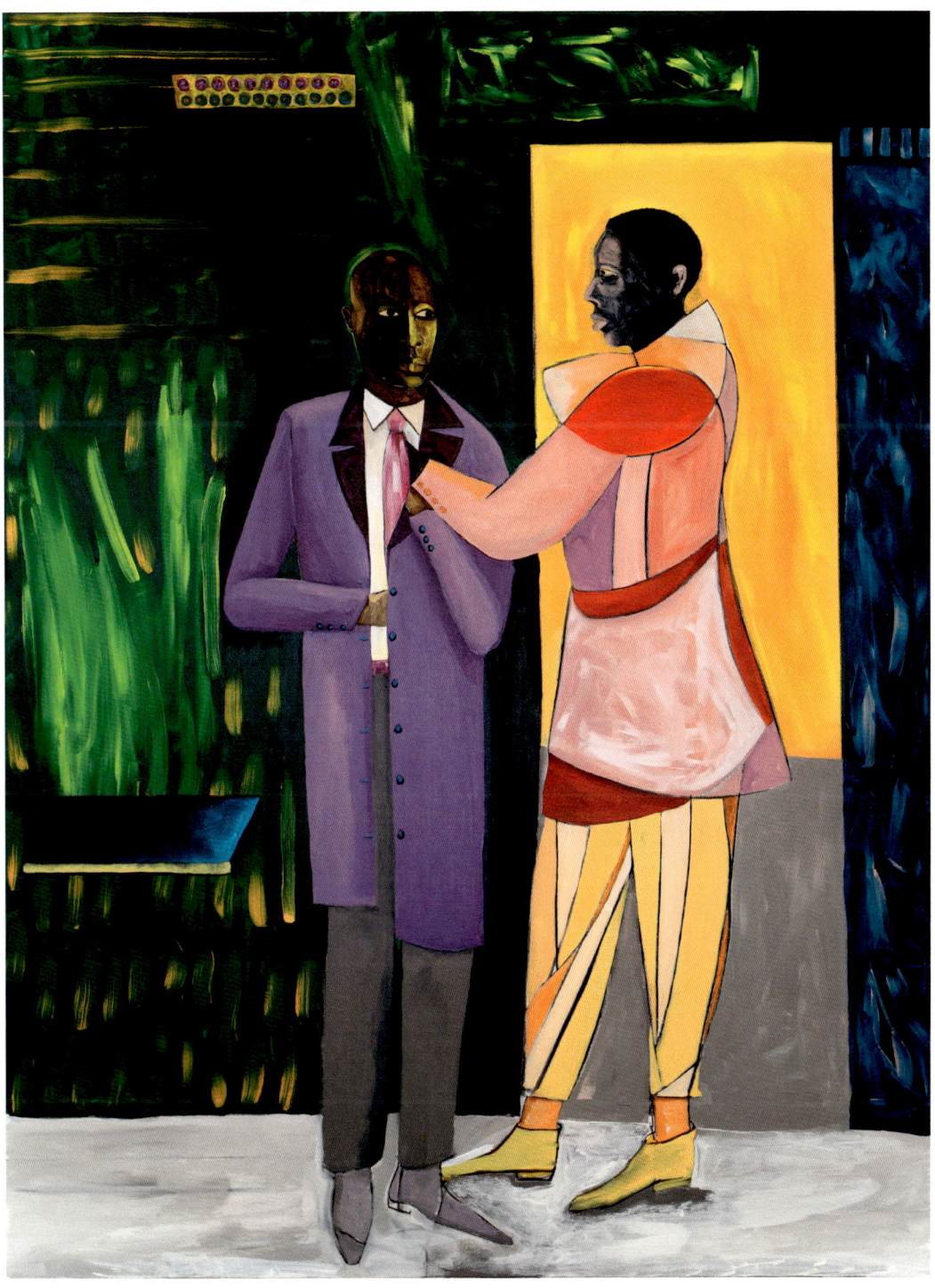

Lubaina Himid, *Favours For Years To Come*,
from the series *How Can I Help You?*, 2025

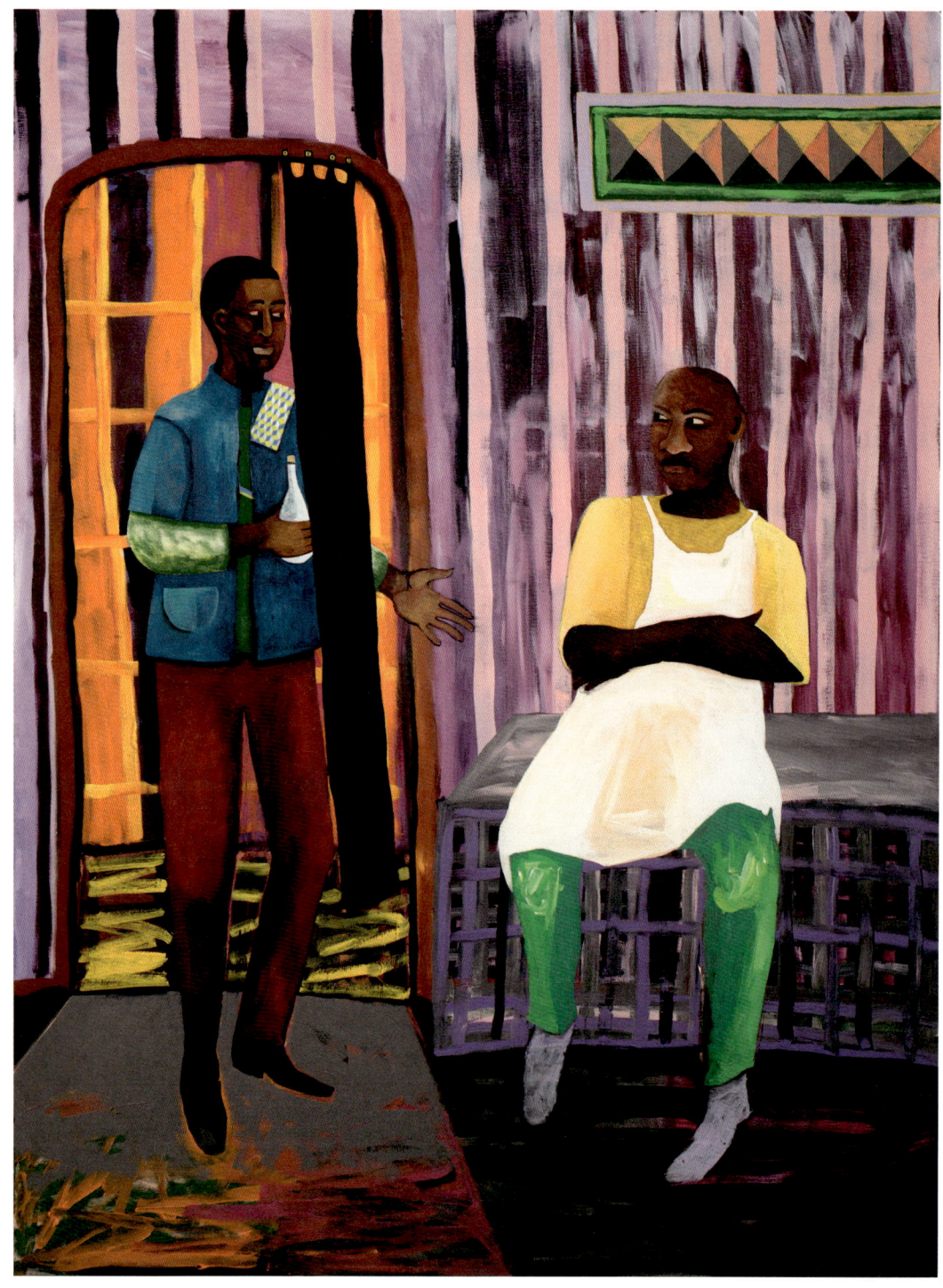

Lubaina Himid, *Repair Jobs*,
from the series *How Can I Help You?*, 2025

3
Repair Jobs

E. Speaking

Ah hello again sorry to be so long finding this, I knew
I had one tucked away somewhere but couldn't quite
remember where I had put it. Thank you for waiting.
I appreciate it. It is good to see you this week. Ah
my friend you look as if you have had a hard day or
perhaps you don't feel too well? But no worries this
will help. I have plenty of time to sit with you and
listen to you. No one else will come around for another
hour or so. Do you want me to get another glass, I can
even find a small tasty something for you to eat if you
have time. You can do a couple of repair jobs for me
if you are short of money, there is always something to
fix in this funny little place.

F. Thinking

Yes, I am tired and unhappy but need to look angry,
especially in front of you.

    I desperately need company, a spot of wine and
small amounts of food tenderly offered but am so
exhausted from doing paid work, all over the city, that
this offer is going to be almost impossible to take up.
I wonder whether I can explain this without crying.

E. Thinking

Damn I've gone too far and should have taken it slower
especially with my stupid offer of work in exchange
for wine and food. He looks completely knackered. I
can give him food and wine for nothing and will say
so in one moment as long as he doesn't get up and walk
away now.

F. Speaking

Thank you I like this place and would be happy to
fix a few things for you occasionally in exchange for
some friendly conversation, some fine wine and your
delicious snacks.

Your Charm Offensive

G. Speaking

Look mate I really appreciate how much you like the
stuff I sell but I can't keep giving it to you for
nothing. You consistently dress better than me and
your fabulous shoes are newer than mine. You may be
surprised to learn that I really need to make a proper
living. I have people to support and ideas for the
future. Yes, I know you tell everyone how good my stuff
is but your charm offensive doesn't pay my bills. Yes,
I know, it truly does look impressive to everyone who
knows you or catches a glimpse of you walking away with
armfuls of my goods. Yes, it's true, this does seem to
attract more customers but never enough to balance the
books. I keep wondering what on earth I can do to get
this relationship back on an even keel but nothing I
seem to do or say to you is making any difference.

H. Thinking

Idiot.

G. Thinking

He thinks I'm an idiot.

H. Speaking

O.K. I'll go somewhere else, to help another business
nearby that sells the same stuff as you but has always
been willing to let me have it for free.

G. Thinking

Idiot.

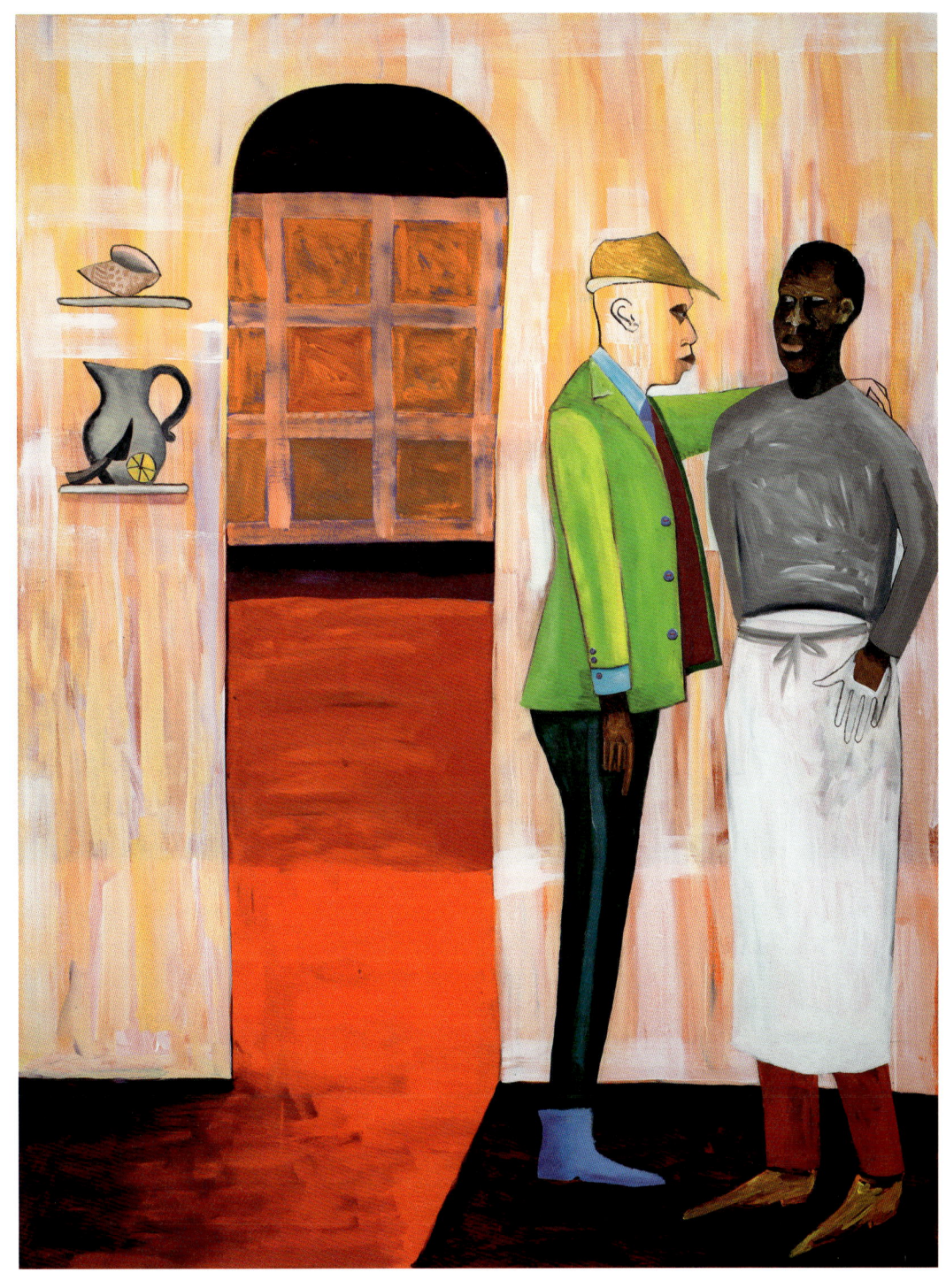

Lubaina Himid, *Your Charm Offensive,*
from the series *How Can I Help You?*, 2025

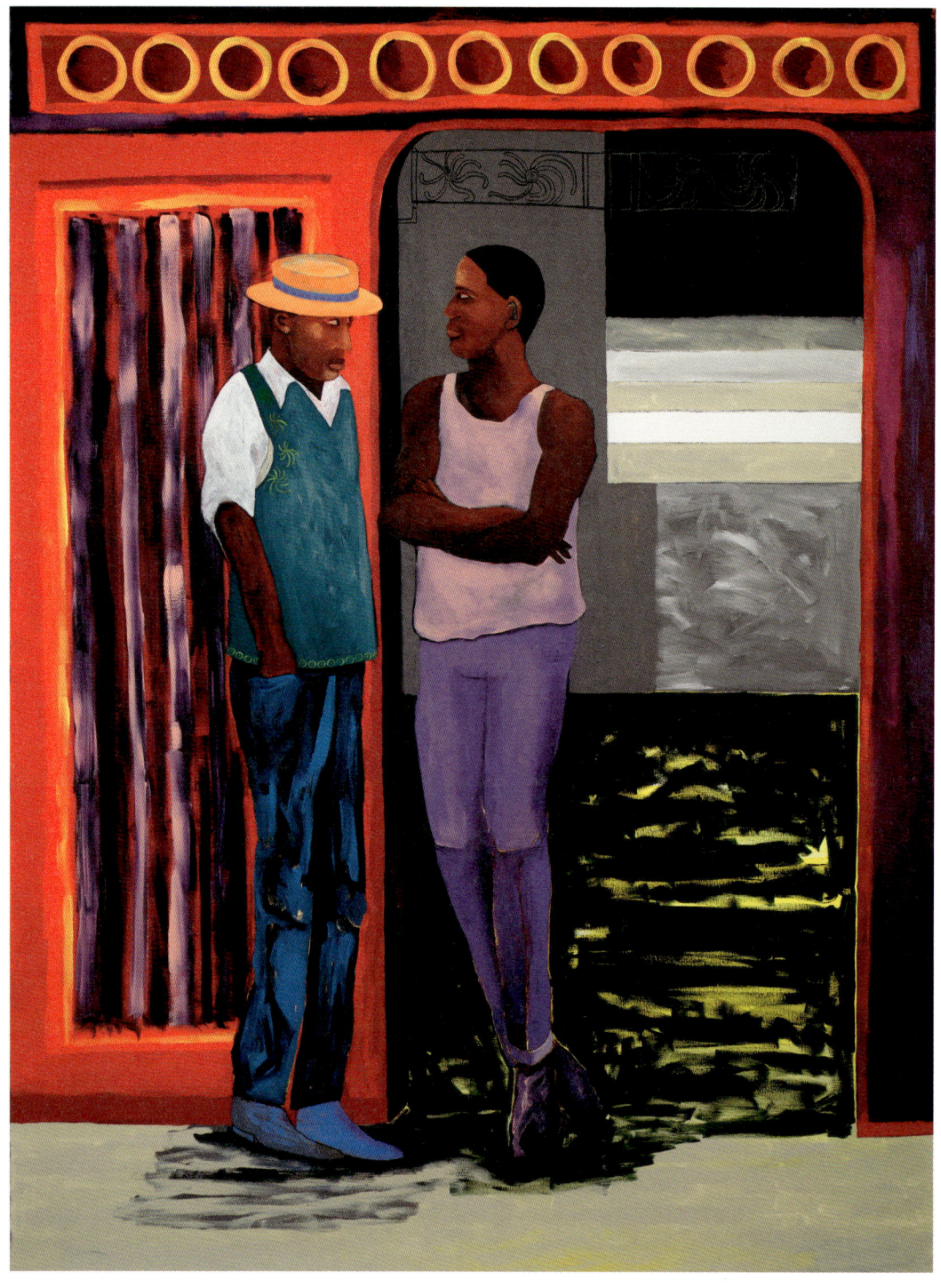

Lubaina Himid, *Try Out a Few of Them,*
from the series *How Can I Help You?*, 2025

5
<u>Try Out a Few of Them</u>

I. Speaking

Hello again! Nice to see you! Strangely I really like
the way you just show up here wearing very little and
spend a huge amount of time looking at what I've got
for sale. It seems funny though that you never seem to
want to actually buy anything. I don't really mind;
you are very charming but it would be good to know
whether you keep coming back here because you can't
see anything you like despite the huge selection or
whether you simply don't know what you want. From your
conversation I get the feeling that you are trying
to impress someone and think that my shop holds the
key to this. However, unless you tell me what you are
looking for and what the occasion you are attending
actually is, it will be hard to know how to guide you.
I do understand that you need a hat and that when you
obviously never wear them, this can be a problem but I
still need more information and frankly you need to try
out a few of them on your head not just in your hand.

J. Thinking

I simply want to spend time with you my friend.

I. Thinking

Calm down.

J. Speaking

I'd like to buy the one you are wearing.

If you would like to come and

Alors viens ite! Dis

and some weeks with me — come — and at once.

moi quand tu viens   exactement —

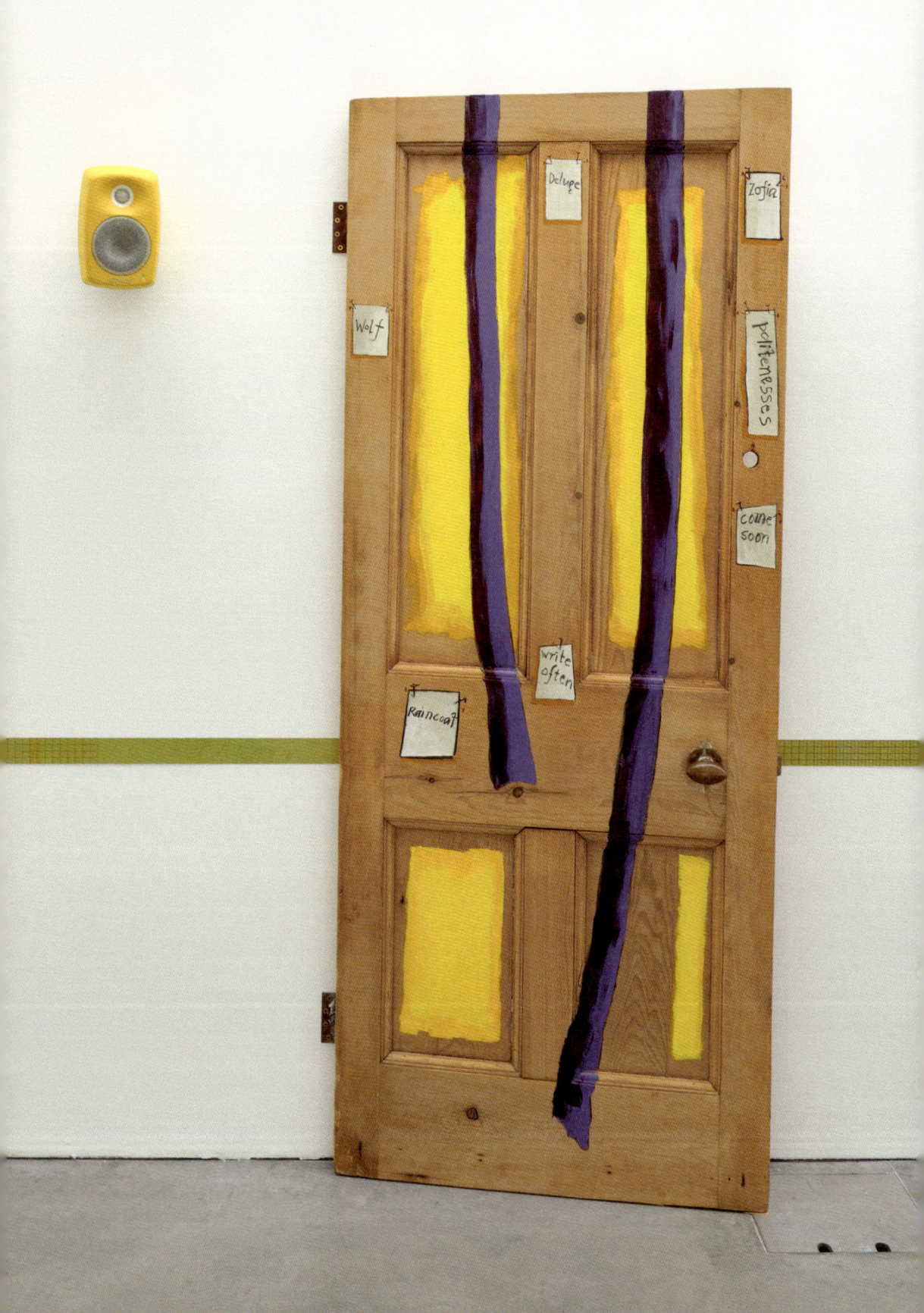

Dear Magda,

There are several things it seems important to say
about the history of the work we are doing together
for Kettle's Yard, but I need to know whether you see
it in the same way as me. This collaborative project
is so different from our separate practices yet there
are conversations between the texts, the materials, the
motifs and the life experiences that we have both lived
through which while very different are almost bizarrely
similar. The way this visual and audio partnership has
grown and transformed during the past few years since
we made *Blue Grid Test* in 2020 for WIELS in Brussels,
surprises me every time I try to pin down what we
have done.

I attempt occasionally to track chronologically how
our everyday exchanges and studio interweaving morphed
into being an independent mode of working, thinking
and making that's quite different from our separate
practices. We seem to have crafted and honed a multi-
disciplinary layered narrative that is quite unique but
often misunderstood by curators and gallerists. Museum
visitors and gallery audiences on the other hand seem
time and again to totally understand what is going on.

Slightly Bitter, made for Kettle's Yard, is essentially
a conversation about chance encounters. That process
of us thinking and reading and talking a great deal
about Zofia Gaudier-Brzeska and Nina Hamnett made me
think about how dealing with the difficulty of hanging
on to who you are can just as easily slip into a world
in which one cannot remember how to care properly for
oneself or others. I felt very comfortable and reassured
as you made silkscreen prints on paper and on linen,
tiny moving image works and the sound composition. It
gave me the confidence to make paintings on objects
and small canvases, and at the same time think about
our postcard collage. It was fun and intriguing to
work separately but in adjoining studios. We borrowed
each other's motifs, we worked over and added to the
surfaces of each other's work while figuring out tiny
problems connected to love and togetherness.

The letters between Nina and Zofia are a minute part of both their lives and only exist because of their completely different relationships with Henri Gaudier-Brzeska. We built on these by talking about the weather, language, as well as letter and postcard communications between us. We invented conversations based on Zofia's letters to Nina, narratives from Zofia's *Matka* and anecdotes taken from Nina's *Laughing Torso*. We worked on and with several layers and levels of communication exploring memory, experience, language, pronunciation, name changes and multiple identities.

I feel that we couldn't have done it without this long history of working together; recently as partners and for twenty years or so as participants in each other's work. The full list of our 'collaborative over-layering' is quite significant now. It's true that *Naming the Money*, *Reduce the Time Spent Holding* and *Old Boat, New Weather* are all enormous projects, that were conceived very differently — I need someone somewhere (an art historian probably) to interrogate what exactly we were doing in making these works between 2016 to 2019. Our collaboration seemed to come together in a rather casual way with me feeling free to say what I wanted you to do without really understanding what a huge difference it was making to my thinking and my practice. Once I had understood better how to work together and in a more egalitarian way these projects gave me a renewed energy for making work and living my life. *Old Boat, New Weather* is a conversation about a long and intermeshed history of the exploitation of people and the environment. However, one of the most important elements of our time working in the print studio on this edition was that I began to understand more about transparency, viscosity and how colour, when applied through the method of silk screen printing doesn't have to have a name to exist.

Alla Prima/Cross Hatch started with a conversation about the history of printmaking and the possibilities of multiple reproductions. We were marvelling at the engraving technique of William Hogarth, and then decided to push water-based etching ink to its limits, combining it with silkscreen printing and layering on top of wet on wet acrylic paint. The 24 unique painting/silkscreen prints are one of the most exciting series of work I have made with you simply because your understanding of and expert control over what would happen to the surfaces during the process of making, was like being with a magician.

Blue Grid Test is a conversation about love and what it sounds like. For this work we conversed about language, discussing the differences between translation and interpretation, which led us to discover our passion for codes and patterns. The full story of how it came into being is forever tied up with working in isolation together during the covid-19 pandemic, when we were recording, collecting and overpainting in the house and studio. Then we showed but never experienced it at WIELS in Brussels. The huge and intricate paper version that was shown at Hollybush Gardens took on the status of your own 'soundless' installation. It is a very special love poem to silkscreen printing, I think.

Zanzibar took several simultaneous conversations about our family histories, our leaving home and our strategies for belonging, in which we spoke of loss and love through guidebooks and radio archive material from twentieth-century British radio programmes. It's a huge project and every time we stage it, I realise how staggeringly important it is, and has become, now that it is a work we have made together.

Street Seller Signs is a soundless sound work in which we discuss the difference between what is said and what is felt. It is a ten-piece optical conjuring trick involving paper disguised as cardboard, ten silkscreened phonetic puzzles and paintings of precious objects. Visitors made the noise themselves sounding the phonetic words out loud while bending and twisting to understand the pain. Of course, because it was displayed at Greene Naftali in New York, it no longer exists as a whole work but is split into fragments held in museums and private collections. I know that you know all this history and have so much to say from your own perspective about each work we made together — so maybe write to me whenever you can and let me know what has been left out and what you were feeling about the effort of collaborating, the balance of authorship, and the relationships of some of these installations to your own practice.

Love,
Lubaina

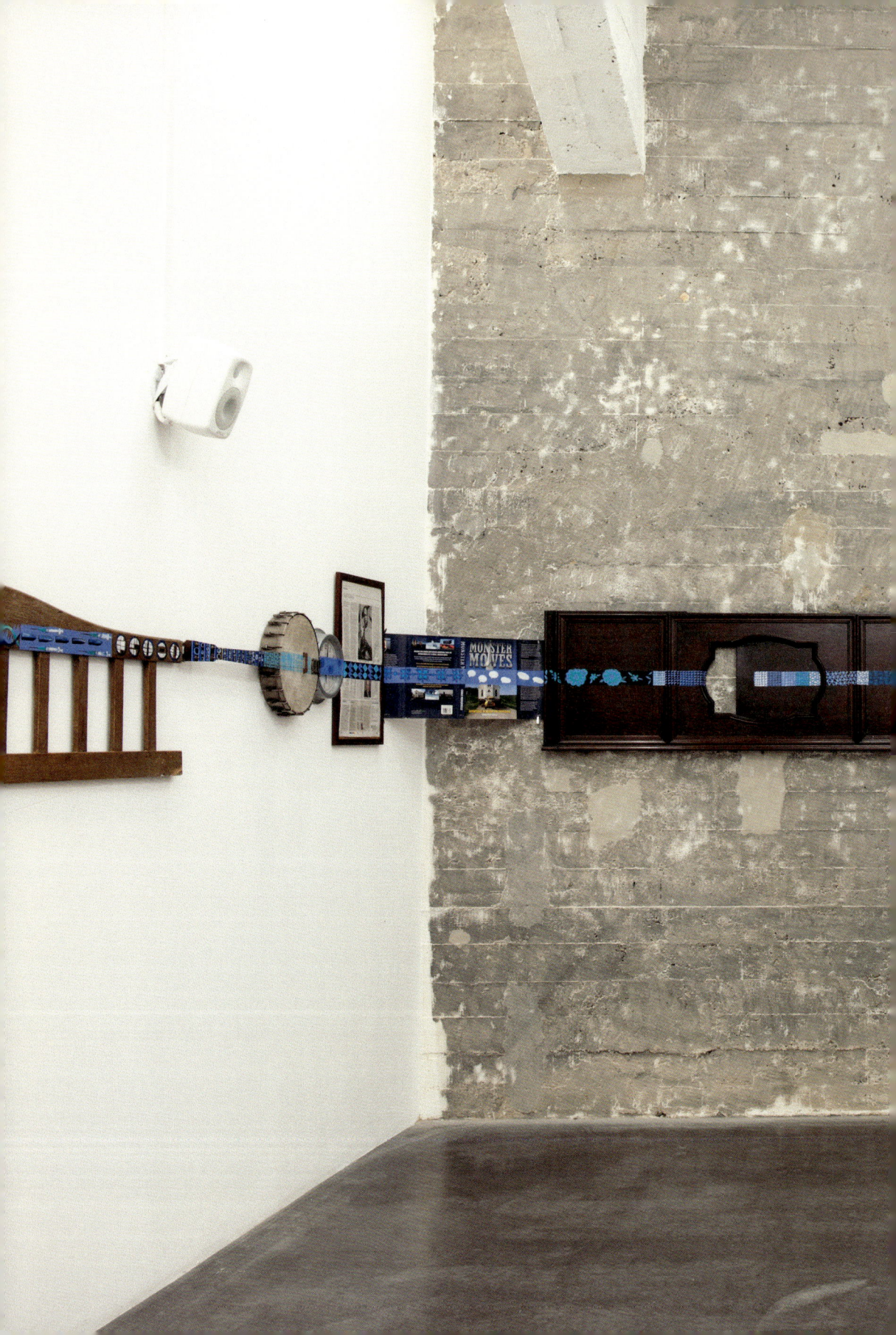

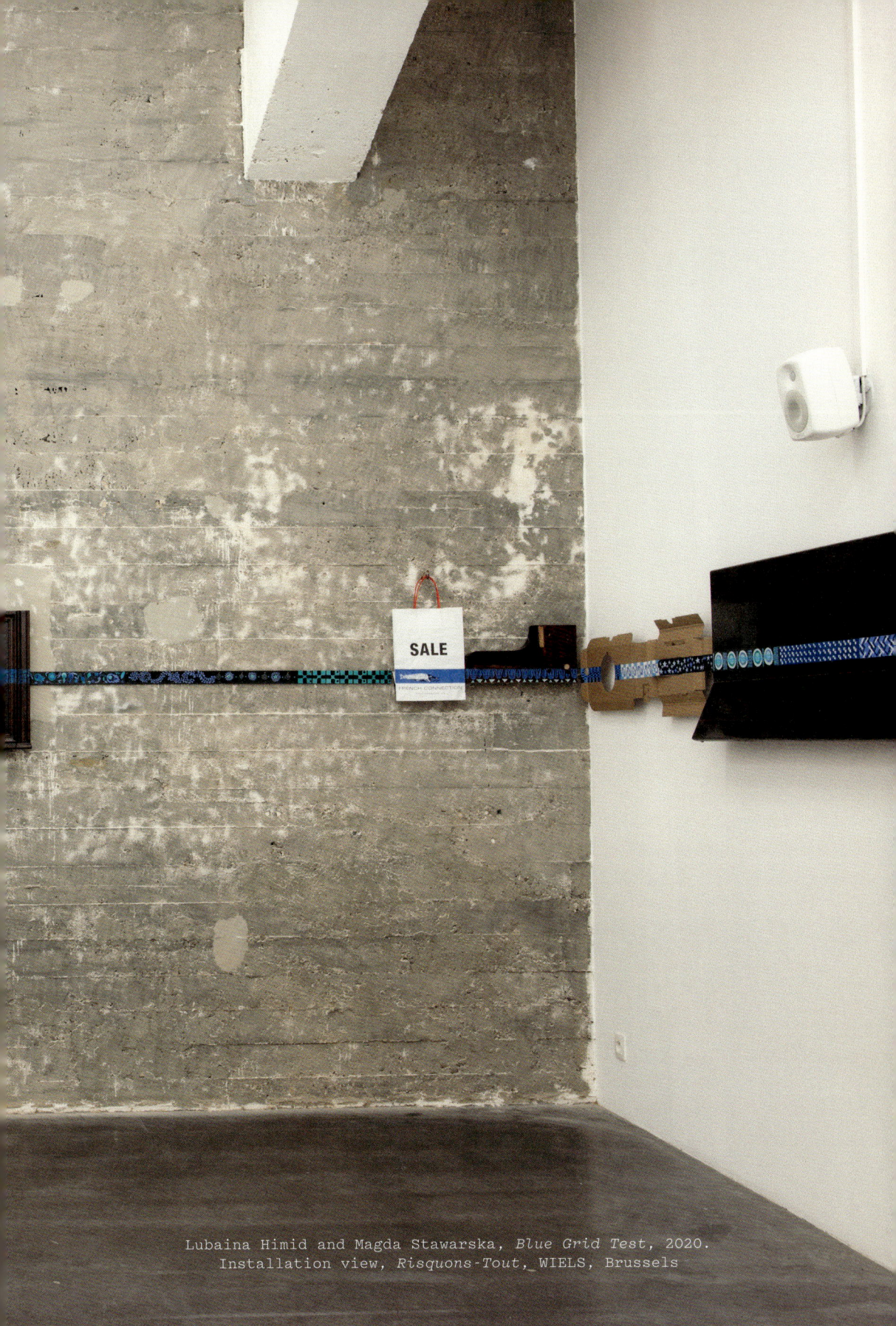

Lubaina Himid and Magda Stawarska, *Blue Grid Test*, 2020.
Installation view, *Risquons-Tout*,_WIELS, Brussels

<u>**Brussels, 5 April 2025**</u>

Dear Magda,

Thank you for sending me the book by Zofia Gaudier-
Brzeska — I read it the very day it arrived. I have
come across the film *Savage Messiah*, which also tells
the story of Zofia and Henri. While the book provides a
dramatic account of a woman who — fleeing her oppressive
family and a forced marriage — finds herself a social
outcast, condemned to loneliness and eventually, an
asylum, the film struck me as a rather grandiose tale
about the relationship between a genius artist and an
emotionally unstable woman, a wannabe writer.

    I have chosen the format of a letter here,
referencing your new work and the correspondence
between Gaudier-Brzeska and Nina Hamnett, but above all,
because this is an opportunity for me to return to our
conversations, for which we now have so little time. The
context of Gaudier-Brzeska's letters may seem distant,
but there are themes that resonate with our own story —
struggling with the reality of life abroad, friendship,
and what Lubaina refers to as 'negotiating unbelonging'.

    The letter format feels more fitting; I would find
it awkward to write a piece of curatorial critique
about your works. I don't feel sufficiently detached
from them, especially the early ones, which you created
while I was hanging around in your studio for hours on
end, and which were simply a part of my everyday life.

    When I saw your new works at the exhibition at
Keiko's, I was struck by how deeply they moved me. I
think this was because I had once watched your prints
unfold — layer by layer — as you prepared each screen,
while we talked about everything and nothing. For a
while, they were simply part and parcel of the bustle
in the studio — amid the silkscreens, the works of
students, and the artists from the ArtLab. For me, your
exhibition works had already become familiar, a given.

    The works at Keiko's were recognisably very
'yours', yet somehow distant. Large paintings and
screenprints depicting old boats and fishing nets, with
intricately applied patterns. Slides with afterimages
from Sharjah, interspersed with poetic text, projected
onto cascading rolls of delicate Japanese paper. The
installation was ephemeral, poetically nostalgic,

unsettling. I found myself wondering where this unease came from.

You and I once talked about the patterned painting rollers, popular in Poland back when we were both children; they were meant to imitate wallpaper, hard to come by at the time. The patterns in your prints at Keiko's reminded me of the roller-painted patterns on the walls of my grandmother's house. At first, I thought that perhaps my emotions stemmed from an unexpected return of these childhood memories. But then I remembered your other works – that unease was already present there. In your curtain piece, with its almost Lynchesque ambience, in the cut-up print with the doors of the Berlin synagogue, in your works from Łódź, in the veiled façades of buildings.

In the boat painting and the prints with fishing nets, you cover the surface with a delicate, ephemeral mesh of floral patterns, creating a tension – a rift – in contrast with the theme of the works: the traces of the fishermen's lives found in Sharjah. I've never been to Sharjah, but it reminded me of Dubai or Abu Dhabi – the meticulousness with which the nouveau riche opulence erases all traces of poverty. It gave the impression of a hallucination. The boats and fishing nets evoke a different reality, a discord within the glossy paradise and the promise of luxury vacations.

It occurred to me that these patterns, in a sense, function as an instruction – they draw attention to the surface of the painting; you have to get closer to examine them. The gaze glides over the floral patterns, then onto the texture of the painting, the grainy surface of the print, and the paint applied to it. The image breaks down into abstraction. This focus on detail and the reference to the surface, which unravels the work, seem to say: don't be fooled by the aesthetics and artistry of this intricate composition – behind it hides an uncomfortable reality.

The works pivot on this tension between form and content. I see this most clearly in the print of a synagogue gate in Berlin: the delicate, lacy form shimmering with shades of blue has been slashed into vertical strips – hanging down from it, wilted. Here, you have literally destroyed the print and negated the aesthetics of the form – in the face of the tragic fate of the Jewish community. This is an unequivocal statement that finding a form to address this part of history is impossible.

There are many references to Jewish fate in your works – which is, of course, hardly surprising. Our generation had to face the cruel and formerly carefully concealed parts of our history, when, after the fall of communism, with regained access to archives and research possible once again, horrific events from the past began to surface.

The ethos of the heroic Pole, and our country's perennial claim to being the 'Messiah of Nations' in its struggle for freedom – 'ours and yours' – was crumbling before our very eyes. We came to realise that everything we had been fed in the official narrative was a pack of lies, drenched in a communist-patriotic sauce. Our favourite TV serial, *Four Tank Men and a Dog* – a heart-warming, patriotic wartime tale of brave Poles and noble comrades – the go-to staple of TV in the People's Republic of Poland – was full of historical distortions, just like our history textbooks.

Perhaps that's why I feel there is a certain distrust of representation itself in your paintings – with their fragmentation and unsettling absence. The references to the history of the Jewish community in Poland are sometimes explicit, but often discreet, hard to catch – such as fleeting glimpses of snapshots of the city, fragments of synagogues, old shop signs, or conspicuously empty, ruined sites where buildings once stood.

In *Spaces and Moments*, you visit places and 'non-places', remnants of the Jewish Łódź: a funeral home, a cemetery with barely visible gravestones, submerged

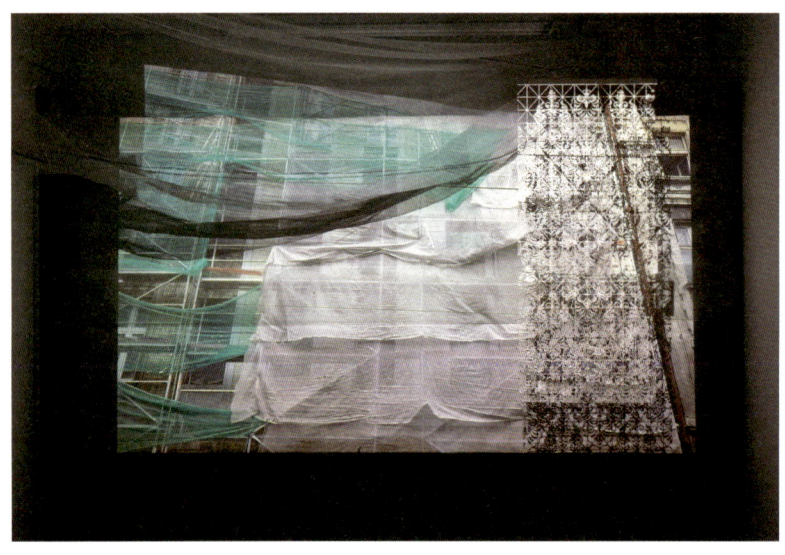

Magda Stawarska,
Ida, 2024, in
Drift, 2024

in unraked leaves. In your video works, you point the camera at the breaches in the city that speak of loss – places where synagogues once stood, now replaced by a parking lot and a square for walking dogs.

The videos are projected onto paper works: sketches with a plan of a demolished synagogue and a watercolour depicting its façade. The synagogue on the old city map and its main walls on the synagogue floorplan – both outlined in red – seep through the video like bloodstains.

In another video work, you are seen stitching – with an old Singer sewing machine – through photographs, printed on soft paper, with afterimages of the Jewish Łódź. The main installation consists of horizontal prints with fragments of the interior of a funeral home – cut up and suspended on a wooden frame. The exhibition is fragmented; empty spaces speak volumes. As do the works themselves.

Here, yet again, the nostalgic, elegiac form in shades of sepia has been negated by the ferocity of cut-up prints, the punctured photographs, the image of a mezuzah scraped off a wooden door – the oppression of oblivion and enforced amnesia.

Grids and patterns run through both your earlier and newer works. The several metres long, horizontal rolls with printed grids and patterns span the main section of the exhibition at MUDAM. When you gave me a tour of the exhibition, one of the visiting curators asked about their meaning (maybe it was more of a 'where did this idea come from' type of question). You spoke about your fascination with maps and patterns, saying that this grid is somewhat like a map, with motifs drawn from various places, from Andalusian azulejos to traditional Indian patterns. It made me think of a kind of cartography of the past, or a musical score, recording the compositions encountered – sounds, rhythms, tonalities.

You have often spoken about these patterns and how applying successive layers is a singular process, because each new layer, each additional element, shape, or colour, completely changes the whole, which is more than the sum of these parts. I thought about the constant having to tell one's story, which living abroad forces upon us. How many times have I had to tell 'my story', when asked, 'Where are you from?' – patching together some kind of coherent narrative out of a series of circumstances or however rashly made, decisions, ambitions, and things we felt we had to do.

Each time, the final 'pattern' turned out a little differently – although the facts had seemingly remained the same, the whole, the composition, the tonality, the spaces between the 'facts' differed on each occasion. The very act of superimposing these successive layers of one's story one upon another, in an account compulsively repeated in the face of the invasive question 'Where are you from?', shifts them towards fiction – resulting in a new narrative that is unlike the previous versions.

Zofia Gaudier-Brzeska, too, wrote about the many versions of her story she maintained for the purpose of her life abroad. By the way, it's interesting how difficult it is to reconstruct her life story. This is, paradoxically, one of the bonuses of living 'na obczyźnie' – 'in an alien land' – as living abroad was called back then by waves of historical Polish émigrés fleeing wars and political repression. The old-fashioned phrase, albeit somewhat pompous in its historical and cultural connotations, provides an apt shortcut to the experience of living in a foreign land, where – after all – one does not belong.

Thinking about your works for this text, I noticed how much – especially in the earlier period – there is a reckoning with the experience of 'living abroad' (let's call it that, for lack of a better term). In *Arcade*, the sounds of the old city, recorded in the vaults of Kraków's medieval Cloth Hall, are transposed to the space-time of Preston. The timing of the eight-hour recording has been synchronised with that of Preston. The morning bustle of Kraków's market square, the sound of the trumpeter playing live on the hour from the Basilica tower abruptly cut off mid-note in commemoration of a medieval siege of the city – can be heard at the same hour in sleepy Preston. The two places are very different, but in your topography they overlap.

Similarly, in your works *From Kraków to Venice in 12 Hours* or *EAST {hyphen} WEST* the routes of your journeys certainly have their historical and cultural connections but, it seems to me, that they were first and foremost your personal travels, without any particular objective, searching for similarities and differences in each city, finding common points of reference between places and discovering the unfamiliar. Every so often, in the sounds of the street

71   bustle, indicators of location emerge: fragments
       of conversations in the local language, passenger
       announcements at a railway station, the street cries of
       stallholders at the Istanbul bazaar, or the sounds of a
       ferry crossing the Bosphorus.

       This layering of soundscapes from different cities
       seems an attempt to translate them; you hint at as much
       in the title of your work *Translating the City*. Some
       elements and details easily find their counterparts in
       our topographical-cum-cultural glossary, others do not.
       This moving between cultures, languages, and contexts,
       finding yourself and getting lost, is like an exercise
       in leaving and returning, in being both 'from here' and
       'from there,' although it seems more about leaving than
       about returning.

       In *Chameleophonia* you speak with various British
       accents, commenting on how accent – especially in
       the British context – places and defines us: where
       we come from, our social status, and so on. When we
       arrive, we try, chameleon-like, to blend into our
       surroundings and learn the language complete with the
       local accent. I remember that while preparing this
       work, you took elocution lessons. I was surprised to
       learn that 'elocution lessons' – an unknown concept in
       Poland – were not something unusual in the UK. Later, I
       understood why. Our 'foreign' accent gives us away with
       the very first sound we utter. Perhaps those we talk to
       can't exactly place where we're from, but it's clear
       we're not 'from here'. Sooner or later, the question
       'Where are you from?' raises its head again.

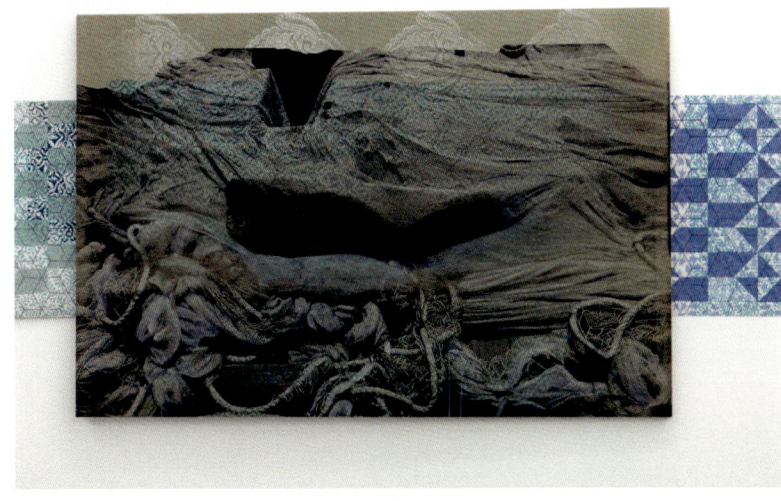

Magda Stawarska,
foreground:
*Littoral
Enfolding*, 2024
and background:
Drift Horizon I,
2024 in *Drift*,
2024.

I read about you as a *flâneuse*, listening to the
city, an attentive observer who disappears from view.
Indeed, you almost never appear in your works yourself.
In the piece of yours I have in my room and look at
every day, and which shows the reflection of a Viennese
street in glass doors, there is a barely perceptible
outline of your own silhouette, but your reflection is
hidden behind the central part of the wooden doors. I
wondered if this 'disappearance', this 'being apart',
isn't part of that limbo between contexts, languages,
and cultural registers that life outside our own
country thrusts us into. I think, for example, about
how I experience the Spanish countryside, where my
faltering Spanish places me in the role of a silent,
voiceless observer. And even though I flatter myself
that I speak English with reasonable confidence, I have
frequently found myself in a situation in England where
my inadequate vocabulary or not getting a cultural
reference has left me outside the conversation.

In Luxembourg, we talked about the 'disappearing'
in your works. Lubaina said at the time that you had
different strategies for 'negotiating unbelonging'.
It's a great way to put it; it also applies to my own
'negotiations' and to the strategies that I notice
in your works. Yes, you both negotiate unbelonging –
in different ways, but together. The 'together' here
is key.

Writing this letter, I thought about how
friendship with the shared experience of being 'from
somewhere else' is singular; it is a microcosm that
doesn't require translation – a micro-family, which,
like a lens, focuses its functions and dysfunctions.
Zofia Gaudier-Brzeska's letters to her friend are full
of desperation; she clings to this friendship as her
only hope, a closeness in a world that is falling apart
around her – it is like love in the time of cholera.

I'm very curious about your new work for Kettle's
Yard. I am coming in a week, so we'll have a chance
to talk.

Hugs to you and Lubaina,
Aneta

Bruksela, 5 kwietnia 2025

Cześć, Kochana,

Dziękuję Ci za przesłaną książkę Zofii Brzeskiej – przeczytałam ją tego samego dnia. Znalazłam też film, *Savage Messiah*, opowiadający historię Zofii i Henry'ego. O ile książka jest zarysem dramatycznej historii kobiety, która uciekając przed opresyjną rodziną i przymusowym związkiem, wyrzucona została poza społeczny nawias, skazana na samotność, a w końcu szpital psychiatryczny, o tyle film wydał mi się mocno egzaltowaną opowieścią o związku artysty-geniusza z emocjonalnie niestabilną, niespełnioną pisarką.

Korzystam z formy listu, nawiązując do Waszej nowej pracy i do korespondencji Brzeskiej z Niną Hamnett, ale przede wszystkim z tego powodu, że ten tekst jest dla mnie okazją, aby wrócić do naszych rozmów, na które teraz mamy tak mało czasu. Kontekst listów Brzeskiej pozornie wydaje się odległy, ale są tam wątki bliskie naszej historii – zmagania z rzeczywistością życia poza krajem, przyjaźń i to, co Lubaina nazywa „negocjowaniem nieprzynależności".

List jest też poręczną formą – trudno byłoby mi napisać kuratorsko-krytyczny tekst o Twoich pracach. Nie mam do nich dystansu, zwłaszcza do tych wczesnych, które powstawały, kiedy godzinami przesiadywałam w Twojej pracowni, i były po prostu częścią mojej codzienności.

Kiedy zobaczyłam Twoje nowe prace na wystawie u Keiko, byłam zaskoczona, jak emocjonalnie je odebrałam. Chyba dlatego, że kiedyś patrzyłam, jak powstają Twoje grafiki – warstwa po warstwie – jak przygotowywałaś kolejne sita, a my rozmawiałyśmy o wszystkim i o niczym. Przez jakiś czas były po prostu częścią krzątaniny w pracowni – pomiędzy sitami, pracami studentów i artystów z ArtLabu. Prace na wystawach wydawały się już opatrzone, oswojone.

Prace pokazane u Keiko były jednocześnie znajome, bardzo Twoje, ale też w jakiś sposób odległe. Duże obrazy i sitodruki przedstawiające stare łodzie i rybackie sieci, z misternie naniesionym na nie wzorami. Slajdy z powidokami z Szardży, przeplatane poetyckim tekstem, projektowane na opadające zwoje delikatnego, japońskiego papieru. Całość efemeryczna, poetycko-

nostalgiczna, niepokojąca. Zastanawiałam się, skąd ten
niepokój.

Rozmawiałyśmy kiedyś o popularnych w Polsce w
czasach naszego dzieciństwa wałkach do malowania
wzorów na ścianach, mających imitować trudno dostępne
wówczas tapety. Wzory na grafikach u Keiko przypominały
malowane takim wałkiem wzory na ścianach domu mojej
babci. Może to emocje związane ze wspomnieniami z
dzieciństwa, które tak niespodziewanie powracają? Ale
przypomniałam sobie Twoje inne prace – ten niepokój
już tam był. W pracy z kurtyną, niemalże Lynchowską
w nastroju; w pociętej grafice przedstawiającej
drzwi berlińskiej synagogi, w pracach z Łodzi, w
zawoalowanych fasadach budynków.

W obrazie z łodzią i grafikach z sieciami
pokrywasz powierzchnię misterną, efemeryczną siatką
kwiatowych wzorów, tworząc rozszczepienie – napięcie
– w zestawieniu z tematem tych prac: śladami życia
rybaków, odnalezionymi w Szardży. Nigdy nie byłam
w Szardży, ale przypomniałam sobie Dubaj czy Abu
Zabi – tę skrupulatność, z jaką nowobogacki przepych
zacierał wszelkie ślady biedy. Sprawiało to wrażenie
halucynacji. Łodzie i sieci rybackie przywołują inną
rzeczywistość, są zgrzytem w folderowym, nowobogackim
raju z obietnicą luksusowych wakacji.

Pomyślałam, że te wzory są w pewnym sensie
„instrukcją" – przywołują uwagę do powierzchni obrazu;
trzeba się zbliżyć, żeby się im przyjrzeć. Wzrok ślizga
się po kwiatowych wzorach, potem po materii obrazu,
ziarnistej fakturze druku, nałożonej na nią farbie.

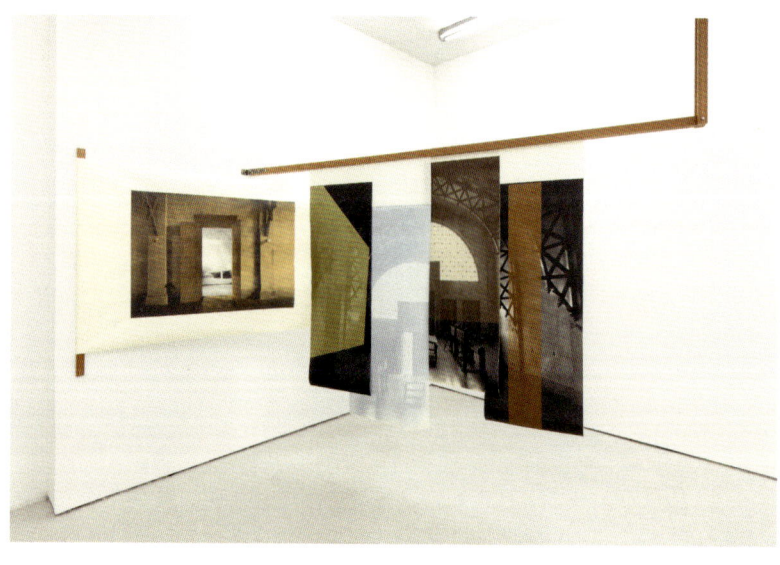

Magda Stawarska,
Bracka 40, 2020
in *Spaces and
Moments*, 2020

Obraz rozpada się na abstrakcję. To skupienie na detalu, odniesienie do powierzchni, podważa narrację; zdaje się mówić: niech cię nie zwiedzie estetyka i kunszt tej misternej kompozycji – kryje się za nią niewygodna rzeczywistość.

Napięcie pomiędzy formą a treścią gra kluczową rolę. Wyraźnie widzę to w pracy przedstawiającej bramę synagogi w Berlinie: delikatna, ażurowa forma mieniąca się odcieniami niebieskiego pocięta jest gwałtownie na wertykalne pasy, które zwisają z niej jakby zwiędnięte. Tutaj dosłownie niszczysz obraz i negujesz estetykę formy – w obliczu tragicznych losów żydowskiej społeczności. Jest to jak kategoryczne stwierdzenie, że znalezienie formy odniesienia się do tej historii jest niemożliwe.

Sporo jest odniesień do żydowskiej historii w Twoich pracach, co oczywiście nie dziwi. Nasze pokolenie musiało zmierzyć się z okrutną i skrzętnie ukrywaną częścią naszej historii, kiedy po upadku komunizmu, wraz z dostępem do archiwów i możliwością prowadzenia badań na jaw zaczęły wychodzić kolejne tragiczne wydarzenia.

Etos bohaterskich Polaków, „Mesjasza narodów" walczącego za wolność „naszą i waszą", rozpadał się na naszych oczach. Zdaliśmy sobie sprawę, że wszystko, co do tej pory serwowano nam w oficjalnym obiegu, było kłamstwem podlanym komunistyczno-patriotycznym sosem. Nasz ulubiony serial *Czterej pancerni i pies* pełen był historycznych przekłamań – podobnie jak podręczniki historii.

Może stąd moje odczucie, że jest w Twoich obrazach jakaś „nieufność" do samej reprezentacji – jej rozszczepianie i niepokojąca nieobecność. Odniesienia do historii żydowskiej społeczności w Polsce są czasem dosłowne, ale często dyskretne, trudne do wyłapania – jak migawki w zdjęciach z miasta, fragmenty synagog, stare szyldy czy puste miejsca po wyburzonych budynkach.

W *Spaces and Moments* odwiedzasz miejsca i „nie-miejsca" pozostałe po żydowskiej Łodzi: dom pogrzebowy, cmentarz z ledwo widocznymi nagrobkami zapadniętymi w nieodgarnianych liściach. W pracach wideo obserwujesz „wyrwy" w mieście – tam, gdzie kiedyś stały synagogi, teraz jest parking i skwer, na którym wyprowadza się psy.

Filmy wideo projektowane są na prace na papierze: szkice z planami nieistniejącej synagogi i akwarelę przedstawiającą jej fasadę. Zaznaczone na czerwono – synagoga na starym planie miasta i jej główne ściany

na rzucie poziomym – prześwitują przez film krwawymi
plamami.

W kolejnym wideo przeszywasz na starym singerze
wydrukowane na miękkim papierze zdjęcia z powidokami
żydowskiej Łodzi. Główna instalacja to horyzontalne
druki z fragmentami wnętrza domu pogrzebowego –
poszatkowane, zawieszone na drewnianej ramie. Wystawa
jest rozczłonkowana, a puste przestrzenie tak samo
wymowne jak prace.

Tu znowu nostalgiczno-elegijna forma w odcieniach
sepii zanegowana jest przez gwałtowność pociętych
druków, przekłutych zdjęć, grafiki z wydrapaną z
drewnianych odrzwi mezuzą – przemoc nie-pamięci i
przymusowej amnezji.

Siatki i wzory przewijają się zarówno w Twoich
wcześniejszych, jak i nowych pracach. Horyzontalne,
wielometrowe zwoje z nadrukowaną siatką i naniesionymi
na nią wzorami spinają główną część wystawy w MUDAM.
Kiedy oprowadzałaś mnie po niej, jeden ze zwiedzających
ją kuratorów zapytał o ich znaczenie (a może było to
pytanie: „Skąd ten pomysł?"). Mówiłaś o fascynacji
mapami i wzorami, o tym, że ta siatka jest trochę jak
mapa, na którą naniesione są motywy napotkane w różnych
miejscach – w andaluzyjskich azulejos czy indyjskich
wzornikach. Pomyślałam, że to jak kartografia
przeszłości albo muzyczna partytura rejestrująca
napotkane kompozycje: brzmienia, tempa, tonacje.

Wiele razy mówiłaś o tych wzorach i o tym, że
nanoszenie kolejnych warstw jest szczególnym procesem,
bo każda kolejna warstwa, kolejne nakładane elementy,
kształty, kolory całkowicie zmieniają całość, która
nie jest po prostu sumą tych elementów. Pomyślałam
o ciągłym „opowiadaniu swojej historii", w co wrzuca
nas mieszkanie poza swoim krajem. Ile razy musiałam
opowiadać „swoją historię", gdy pytano mnie: „Skąd
jesteś?". Klecić jakąś całość z wypadkowej zbiegów
okoliczności czy pochopnie (lub nie) podejmowanych
decyzji, ambicji i rzeczy do zrealizowania. Za każdym
razem ostateczny „wzór" wychodził trochę odmienny -
niby fakty te same, ale całość, kompozycja, tonacja,
przestrzenie pomiędzy „faktami" – za każdym razem inne.
Samo nakładanie kolejnych warstw własnej historii,
kompulsywnie powtarzanej w obliczu tego nachalnego
„Skąd jesteś?", przesuwa je w kierunku fikcji – nowego
opowiadania różniącego się od poprzednich wersji.

Zofia Brzeska też pisała o tym, ile miała wersji
swojej historii na użytek życia na emigracji. Swoją

drogą to ciekawe, jak trudna do odtworzenia była jej prawdziwa historia. To pewnie jeden z przywilejów życia „na obczyźnie", jak zapewne wtedy się mówiło. Pisząc to, zastanawiam się, jak właściwie mówić o tym dzisiaj: „życie na emigracji", „życie za granicą"? Określenie „życie na obczyźnie" obciążone jest skojarzeniami z wielkimi, polskimi emigracjami, rozbiorami, wojnami, politycznymi represjami, a w warstwie słownej bezpośrednio odsyła do „ojczyzny". Czyli wszystko zbyt patetyczne, przyciężkawe, ale „obczyzna" jest jednak świetnym skrótem myślowym odnoszącym się do tego doświadczenia – bycia „na obcym", bycia obcym, wyobcowanym.

Myśląc o Twoich pracach przy okazji pisania tego tekstu, zauważyłam, jak wiele – szczególnie we wcześniejszym okresie – jest w nich rozprawiania się z doświadczeniem „życia poza krajem" (nazwijmy to tak, bo brakuje mi lepszego określenia). W *Arkadach* odgłosy starego miasta, nagrane w podcieniach krakowskich Sukiennic, przenosisz w czasoprzestrzeń Preston. Czas ośmiogodzinnego nagrania, zsynchronizowany jest z czasem w Preston; poranny ruch krakowskiego rynku, dźwięk trąbki z wieży krakowskiej katedry oznajmiający kolejną godzinę, urwany w pół na pamiątkę historycznego wydarzenia – rozlega się o tej samej porze w sennym Preston. Te miejsca są diametralnie różne, ale nakładają się na siebie w Twojej topografii.

Podobnie w pracach *Z Krakowa do Wenecji* czy *Wschód-Zachód* – trasy tych podróży miały swoje historyczne i kulturowe połączenia, ale wydaje mi się,

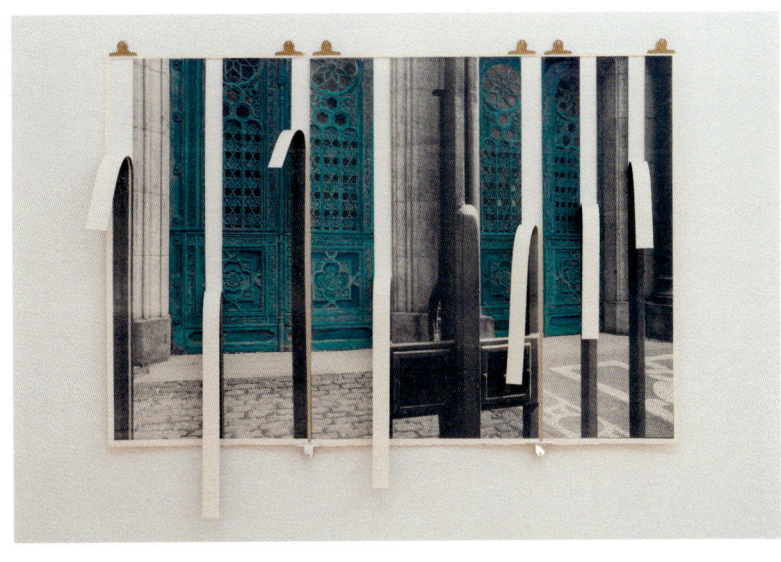

Magda Stawarska,
*Oranienburger
Straße*, 2019

że były to po prostu Twoje podróże, bez większego celu, podczas których szukałaś w kolejnych miastach podobieństw i różnic, wspólnych punktów orientacyjnych, oswajania i różnicowania tych miejsc. Co jakiś czas w dźwiękach ulicznego zgiełku pojawiają się elementy orientacyjne: fragmenty rozmów w lokalnym języku, informacje dla pasażerów na dworcu kolejowym, nawoływania sprzedawców z istambulskiego bazaru, odgłosy promu płynącego przez Bosfor.

To nakładanie na siebie porządków dźwiękowych różnych miast jest jak próba ich przekładania, tak jak w tytule Twojej pracy *Translating the City*. Niektóre elementy i detale łatwo znajdują swoje odpowiedniki w naszym topograficzno-kulturowym słowniku, inne nie. To przemieszczanie się pomiędzy kulturami, językami, kontekstami, odnajdywanie się i gubienie jest jak ćwiczenie w wyjeżdżaniu i wracaniu, w byciu „stąd" i „stamtąd"; chociaż chyba jednak bardziej w wyjeżdżaniu niż w powrotach.

W *Kamelofonii* mówisz różnymi brytyjskimi akcentami, nawiązując do tego, jak akcent – szczególnie w kontekście brytyjskim – umiejscawia nas i definiuje: wskazuje, skąd pochodzimy, jaki mamy status społeczny itd. Przyjeżdżając, próbujemy jak kameleon wtopić się w otoczenie, nauczyć się języka, lokalnego akcentu. Pamiętam, że w przygotowaniu tej pracy brałaś lekcje wymowy, i zaskoczyło mnie, że „lekcje wymowy" nie były czymś niezwykłym w Wielkiej Brytanii. Potem zrozumiałam, dlaczego. „Obcy" akcent zdradza nas od pierwszego dźwięku. Może rozmówcy trudno zlokalizować, skąd jesteśmy, ale wiadomo, że nie „stąd". Prędzej czy później powraca pytanie: „Skąd jesteś?".

Czytam o Tobie jako o słuchającej miasta *flâneuse*, uważnej obserwatorce, która sama znika z pola widzenia. Rzeczywiście, prawie nigdy nie pojawiasz się w swoich pracach. W pracy, którą mam w swoim pokoju i patrzę na nią codziennie, przedstawiającej odbicie wiedeńskiej ulicy w szklanych drzwiach, pojawia się ledwo zauważalny zarys Twojej sylwetki, ale jej odbicie schowane jest za centralną częścią drewnianych odrzwi.

Zastanawiałam się czy to znikanie, bycie obok nie jest częścią tego zawieszenia pomiędzy kontekstami, językami i kulturowymi rejestrami, w które wrzuca nas życia poza swoim krajem. Myślę na przykład o moim doświadczeniu na hiszpańskiej prowincji, kiedy mój kulawy hiszpański sytuuje mnie w pozycji niemej obserwatorki wydarzeń – niemowy. A przecież nawet

znając angielski, przypominam sobie liczne sytuacje w
Anglii, w których brak kulturowych referencji wyrzucał
mnie poza nawias rozmowy.

W Luksemburgu rozmawiałyśmy o znikaniu w Twoich
pracach. Lubaina powiedziała wtedy, że macie różne
strategie „negocjowania nieprzynależności" (*negotiating
unbelonging*). To świetne określenie, które też
mogę odnieść do moich własnych zmagań i strategii,
które odnajduję w Twoich pracach. Tak, negocjujecie
nieprzynależność na inne sposoby, ale wspólnie.
„Wspólnie" jest tu kluczowym słowem.

Pisząc ten list, myślałam o tym, że przyjaźń
we wspólnym doświadczeniu bycia „skądinąd" jest
szczególna; jest mikroświatem niewymagającym
przekładania; mikrorodziną, w której skupiają się
jak w soczewce jej funkcje i dysfunkcje. Listy Zofii
Brzeskiej do przyjaciółki są pełne desperacji; jest
uczepiona tej przyjaźni jak jedynej nadziei na bliskość
w rozpadającym się wokół niej świecie – to jak miłość w
czasach zarazy.

Bardzo jestem ciekawa Waszej nowej pracy do
Kettle's Yard. Będę u Was już za tydzień, więc będziemy
miały okazje porozmawiać.

Ściskam mocno Ciebie i Lubainę,
Aneta

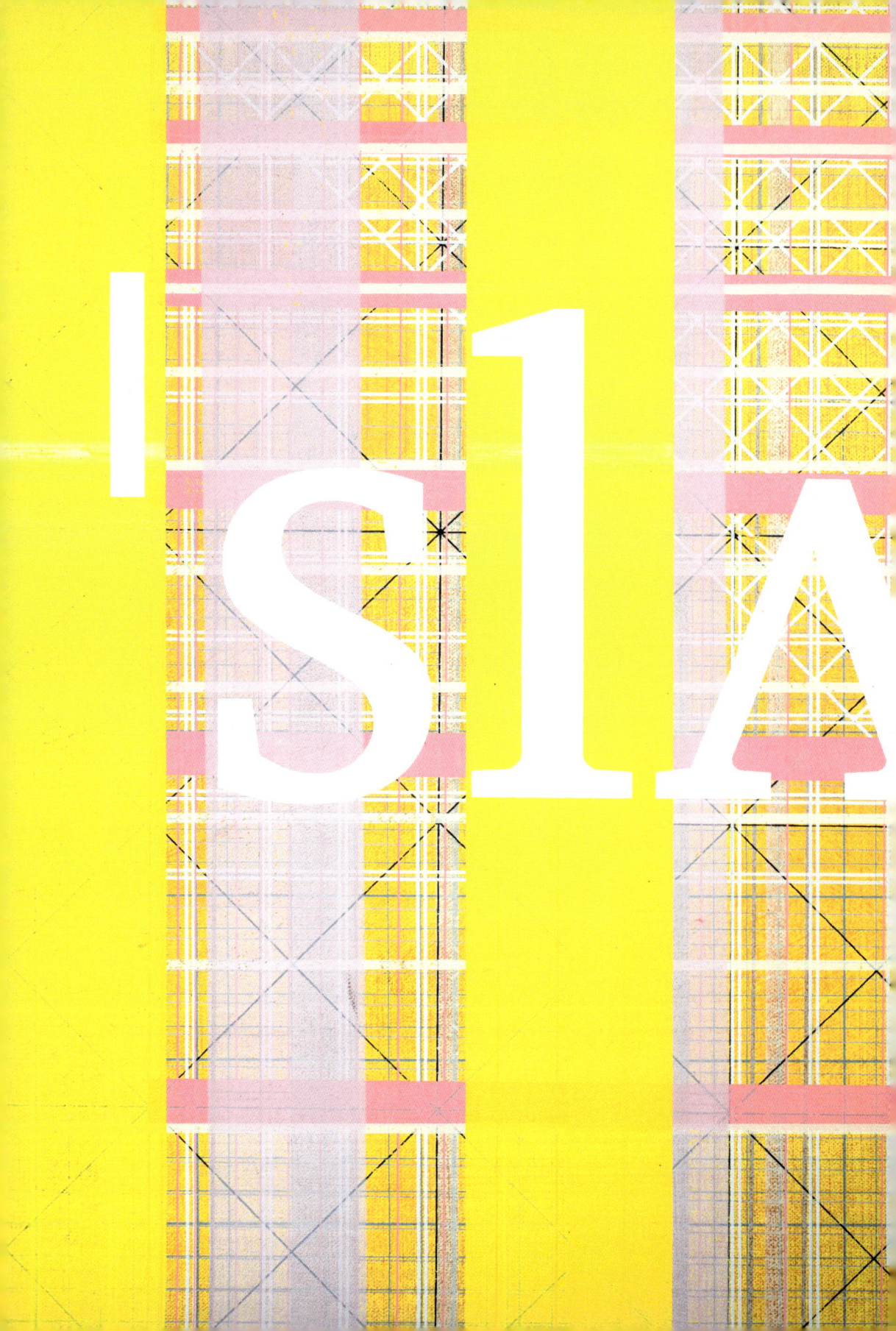

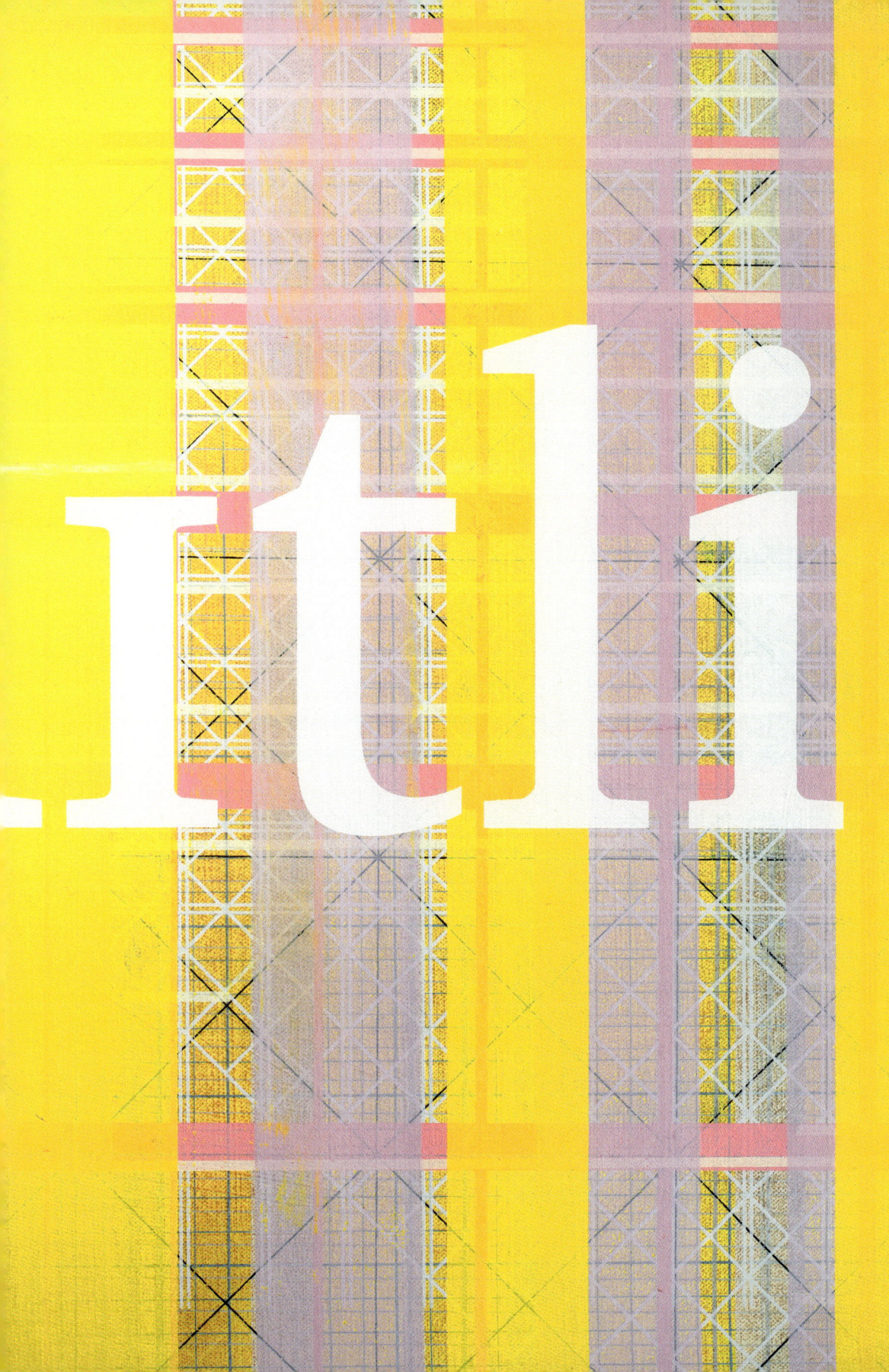

Dear Zofia/Sophia/Zofie,

I hope you don't mind me writing to you out of the blue
like this, but it feels right to let you know what Magda
Stawarska and I are doing with some of the letters
and postcards that you sent to Nina Hamnett during
World War I after Henri had been killed at the front.
Actually, what we are doing is unabashedly using them
to talk about what it means to interrogate prevalent
rules, learned behaviours and unofficial languages
while desperately hanging on to the need to be oneself
while living in a place or space of unbelonging. The
installation is called *Slightly Bitter*.

Magda has read your book *Matka* in Polish and has tried to
understand for herself and explain to me, your strategy
of re-telling, redefining and refining your life history
to suit the circumstances which constantly befell you
as you lurched from one life to another. They called
you mad and locked you up and left you. I have a small
understanding of what people glibly call madness, having
watched a few women that I have known slip relentlessly
towards a state of unravelling, as more than one major
life event melted irrevocably into another.

Between us we examined some of the twists and turns of
your deep but short relationship with Henri and your
brief and rather unsatisfactory encounter with Nina.
Through the making of numerous components — acrylic
and oil paintings on linen and paper, large silkscreen
prints, colour and black and white photographs, tiny
moving image works, and postcard collages we both
sought to communicate our interpretation of the
disconnections between you and the people who failed
to listen to you.

Magda's sound composition surrounds us with fragments
of your letters and plays with pronunciation (and
mispronunciation) in English, French and Polish. We
hear you giving instructions, suffering from illness
and cold, poverty and neglect; there are snatches
of Ravel and audio images of landscape and silence.
Somehow through it all you find the determination to
think about framing Henri's work and selling it to the
right people.

83 When in London we live quite near one of the places you
    may remember, a railway arch in Fulham in which Henri
    used to make work. Magda has taken photographs of it.
    Neither of us have ever been to visit either of the
    small village houses in which you sought the solitude
    to write and which you used as a kind of refuge while
    London was being bombed and where you tried, it seems
    to me very unsuccessfully, to heal the wound of Henri's
    inevitable and sudden death. Sorry we never even tried
    to get there.

    We know you thought of yourself as a poet and a writer,
    but you don't seem to have ever found the time or the
    peace and tranquillity required to spend long hours
    grappling with the creative honing of words in Polish,
    English or French. Your love of *Les Amours Jaunes* the
    poetry collection by Tristan Corbière, who died at age
    29, obviously appealed to you because of its bitter
    wit, and you may be pleased to know that Nina was still
    reading this work aloud to friends, years after you
    introduced it to her when she visited that little house
    you rented from 1916 until 1922 in Wotton-under-Edge.

    Your hunger for intellectual stimulation and constant
    demand to have your ideas reciprocated revealed a great
    deal to us about how horrible it must have been to be
    alone, and in England unable to leave at a time when
    you would rather have been writing in French and living
    among friends in Paris, still poor perhaps but not
    an outcast.

    I am sorry that Nina never had the patience to
    understand your direct way of being yourself or your
    dreadful sense of loss and loyalty in relation to Henri
    and the life you might have lived had he not been
    killed. The fact that you held on to the drawings and
    sculptures that he left in your care and tried to sell
    them only to the best of collectors says a great deal
    about your understanding of how the history of art
    is constructed.

    Mention of your painful teeth, your pleading for a
    decent raincoat and your love of chocolate and rum have
    endeared you to us both.

        Best wishes,
        Lubaina

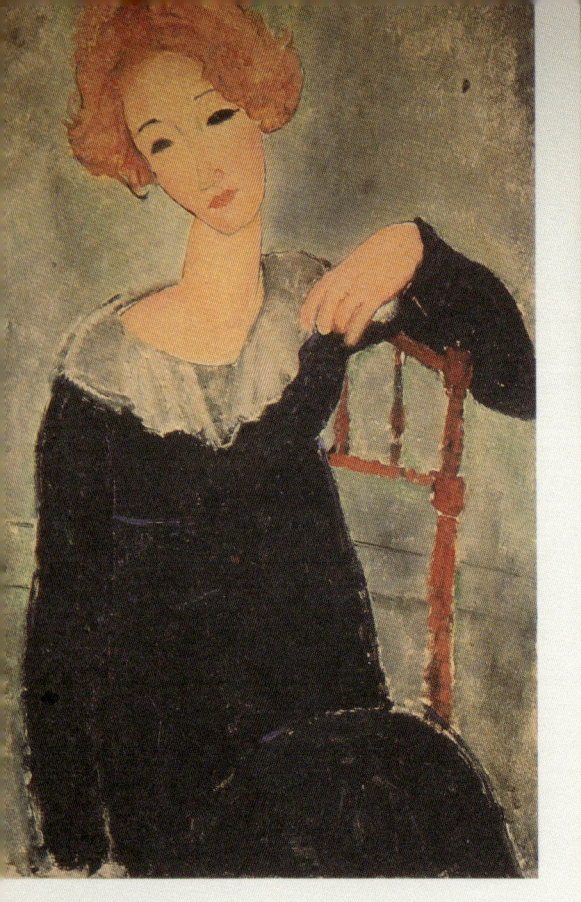
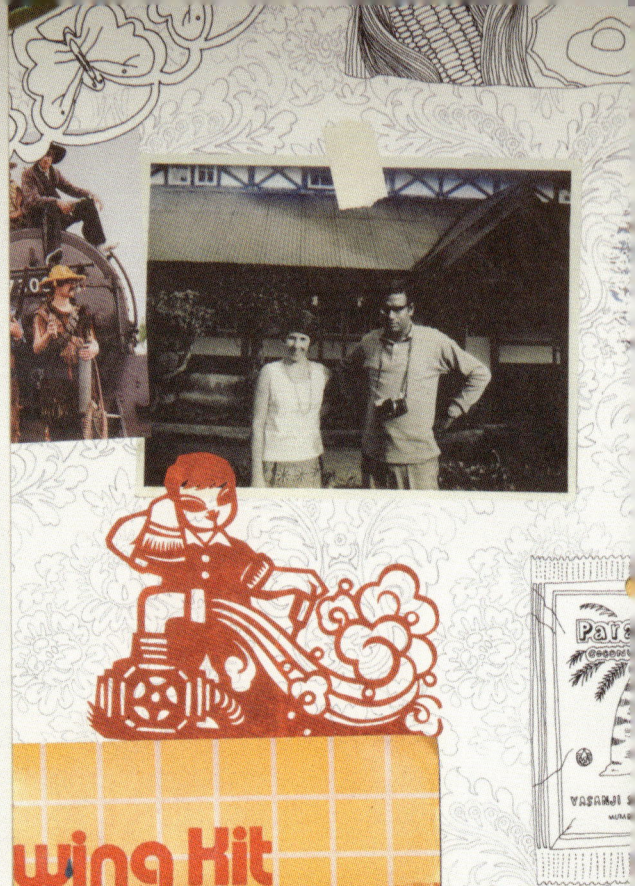
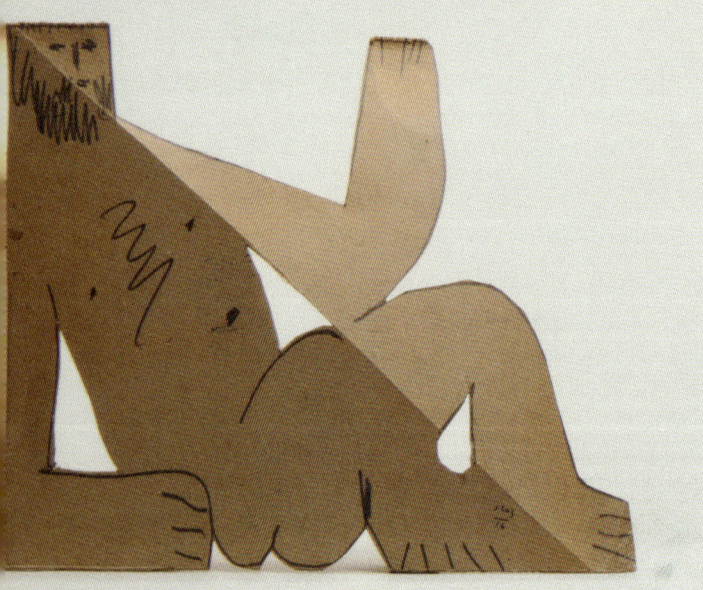

Do women hav
get into th

Less than 4
Art

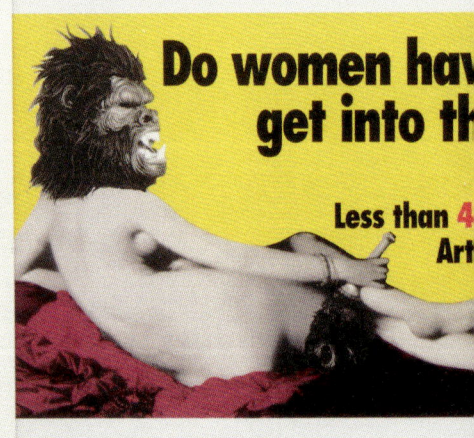
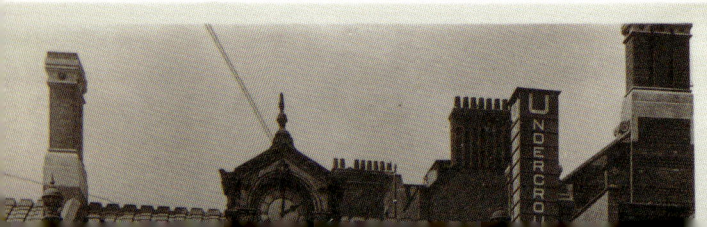
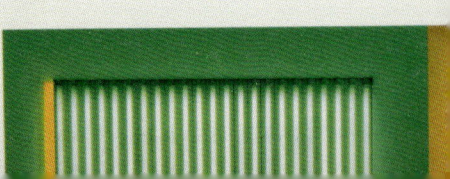

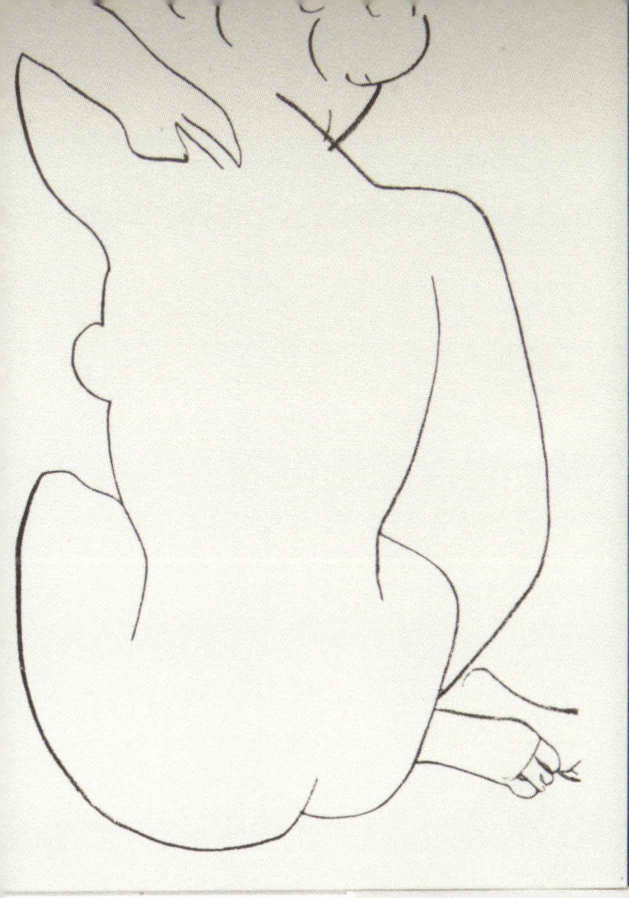

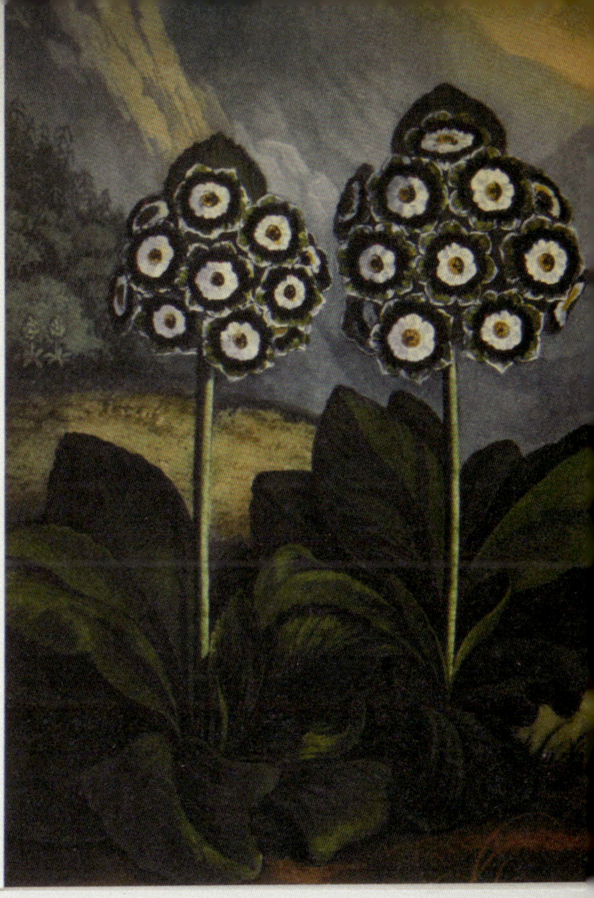

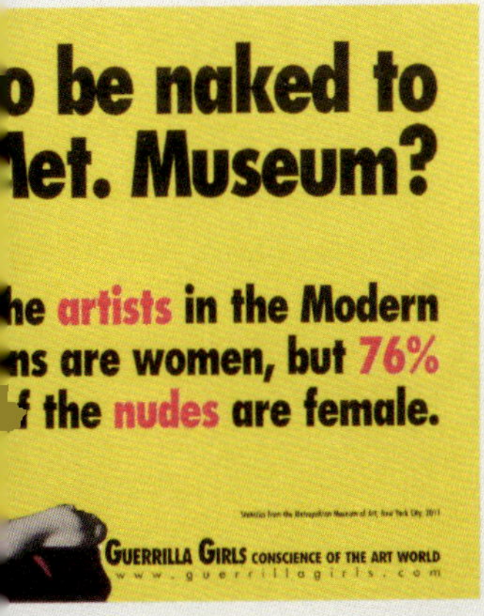

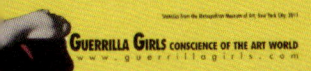

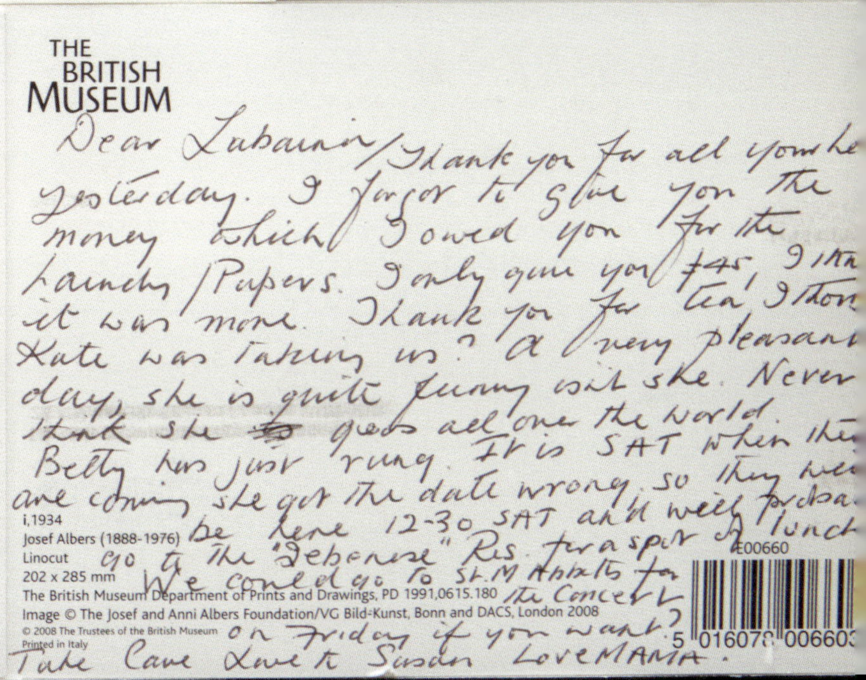

Dear Lubaina / Thank you for all you help
yesterday. I forgot to give you the
money which I owed you for the
Lunches / Papers. I only gave you £45, I think
it was more. Thank you for tea! I think
Kate was taking us? A very pleasant
day, she is quite funny isn't she. Never
think she goes all over the world.
Betty has just rung. It is SAT when they
are coming she got the date wrong, so they will proba-
be here 12-30 SAT and we'll probably
go to the "Japanese" Res. for a spot of lunch
We could go to St. M Abbots for
the Concert
on Friday if you want?
Take Care Love to Susan Love MAMA.

Josef Albers (1888-1976)
i.1934
Linocut
202 x 285 mm
The British Museum Department of Prints and Drawings, PD 1991,0615.180
Image © The Josef and Anni Albers Foundation/VG Bild-Kunst, Bonn and DACS, London 2008
© 2008 The Trustees of the British Museum
Printed in Italy

C10
£00660
5 016078 006603

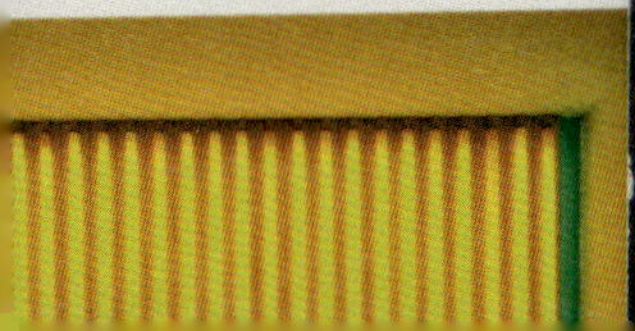

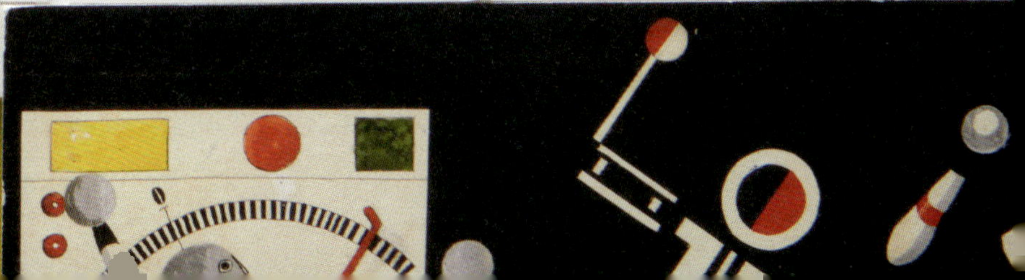

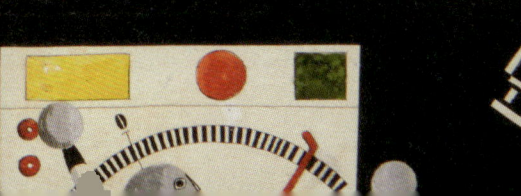

Dear Nina,

I have now read your book *Laughing Torso* three times.
The first time was about thirty years ago when I was
trying to find references to your encounters with Black
people in Paris during and between the European wars
of the twentieth century. The second time was when
I decided to recommend it to readers as part of some
kind of celebrity questionnaire around the time I won
some prize or other; many of your anecdotes which I
read as part of this encounter stalked my mind with no
rest until 2023. My original Virago copy is falling
apart, so when I started this third time, because it
was obvious the reading and notetaking was going to be
quite intense and thorough, I had to buy a new copy.

This time I was looking for every reference you made to
Zofia Gaudier-Brzeska the writer and partner of Henri
Gaudier-Brzeska. In the process it became even clearer
that you are not particularly interested in anyone but
yourself, rather proud of your body and its allure, a
not a very confident artist and a dreadful snob in that
weird and slightly repulsive British way.

You had plenty of lovers and drinking partners
throughout your life, most of whom were artists or
writers. And yes, one of them, for a very short time,
was Henri and so amid your anecdotes about him I can
see what you thought of Zofia.

I'm not sure why you are so rude and dismissive about
this woman, describing her simply as elderly, rather
terrifying and Polish. You said she looked like a
painting of Cezanne's wife, but I presume that this is
because you just cannot imagine why anyone you were
interested in would love someone who wasn't immediately
deemed by you to be attractive — get over yourself, it
happens all the time. It is true that she was needy and
anxious, angry and direct and eventually admitted to an
asylum, but she cared about Henri being remembered as a
good and worthwhile artist.

You are faintly amusing about yourself and your
odd clothes or fancy-dress costumes; dancing to the
Golliwog's Cakewalk in your Apache outfit or donning

'daring for the time' haircuts but again in a weird, distinctly twentieth-century British way. You always describe other people in terms of their nationality and do not bother with their names. Even one of your numerous lovers you describe as 'my Pole'. Other men you describe as 'the abominable Pole' or 'the extremely nice Pole' or 'the other Pole'. Unsurprisingly, you describe a stocking seller as an 'Old Jew', and two artists models as 'a large Negro and his wife'. You talk about 'Russians', 'Spaniards', 'South Americans', and 'the Arab', without saying anything real or personal about them. You describe the hair of the daughter of the President of Liberia as funny, short and woolly. It's painful for me to read.

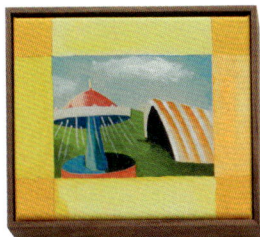

I must confess that I have spent time making what I describe as my 'fake Nina Hamnett paintings'. They are no such things. Mine are predominantly yellow and yours were quite brown and low key. Several of mine depict objects or moments you write about in *Laughing Torso*, and another couple mimic ones you did make, but which I have never seen.

I wanted you to care for Zofia a little and make sure she found opportunities to develop the means to become more able to survive the harshness of unbelonging. Hearing you being amusing about her fear of the moon, when she didn't mention it herself, was disappointing, as was the throwaway description of Zofia and Henri throwing food at each other.

Magda and I wanted to examine our own creative exchanges, our search for a kind of equality — a bolder, clearer means of communication. We used your chance encounter with Zofia, and my chance encounter with your letters and postcards to do it. We didn't set out to catapult you to the high status of genius nor did we think that Zofia's writing was a brilliant example of twentieth-century European literature. However, your lives were extremely interesting, both of you struggling to be yourselves in quite different ways and this resonated with us — so thank you for keeping some of the correspondence between you instead of just throwing it away.

Best wishes,
Lubaina

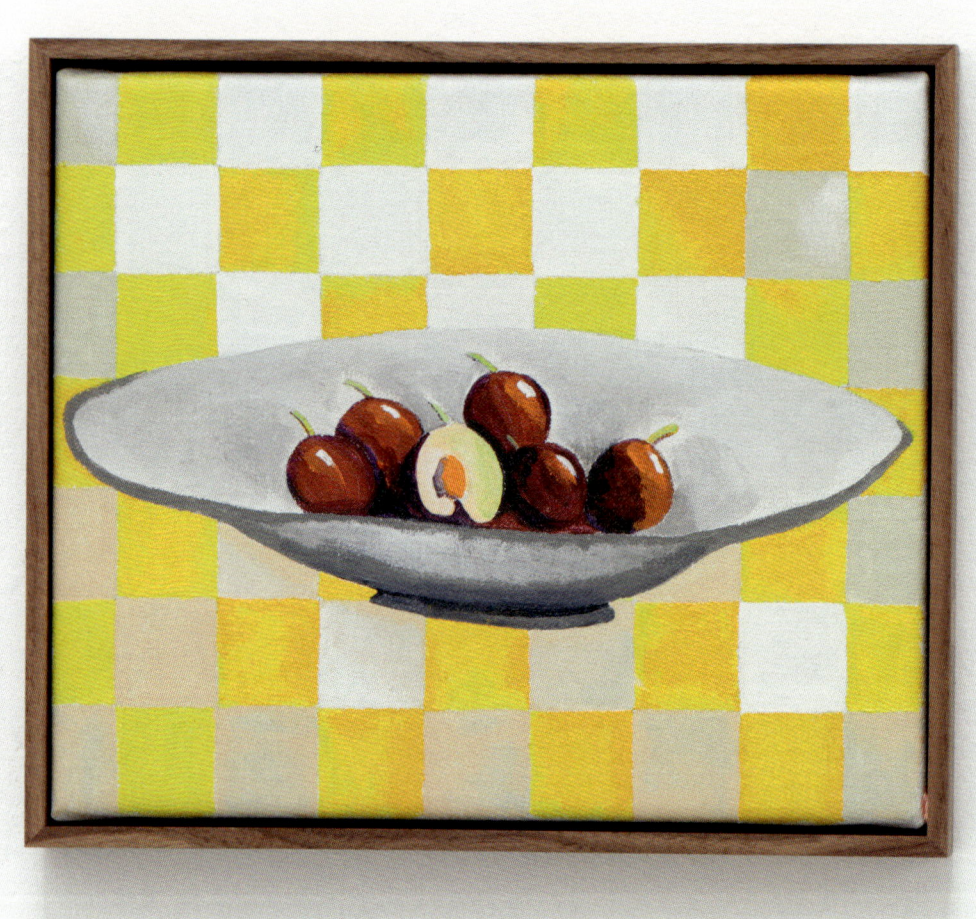

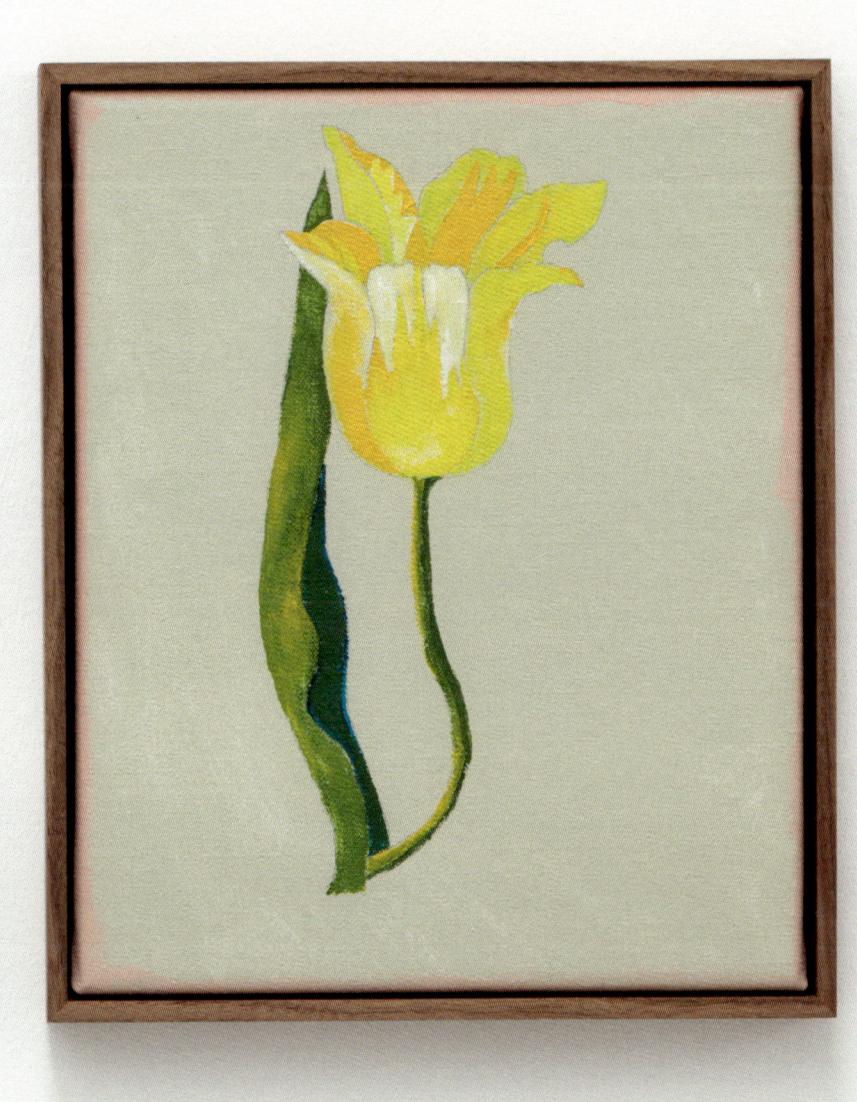

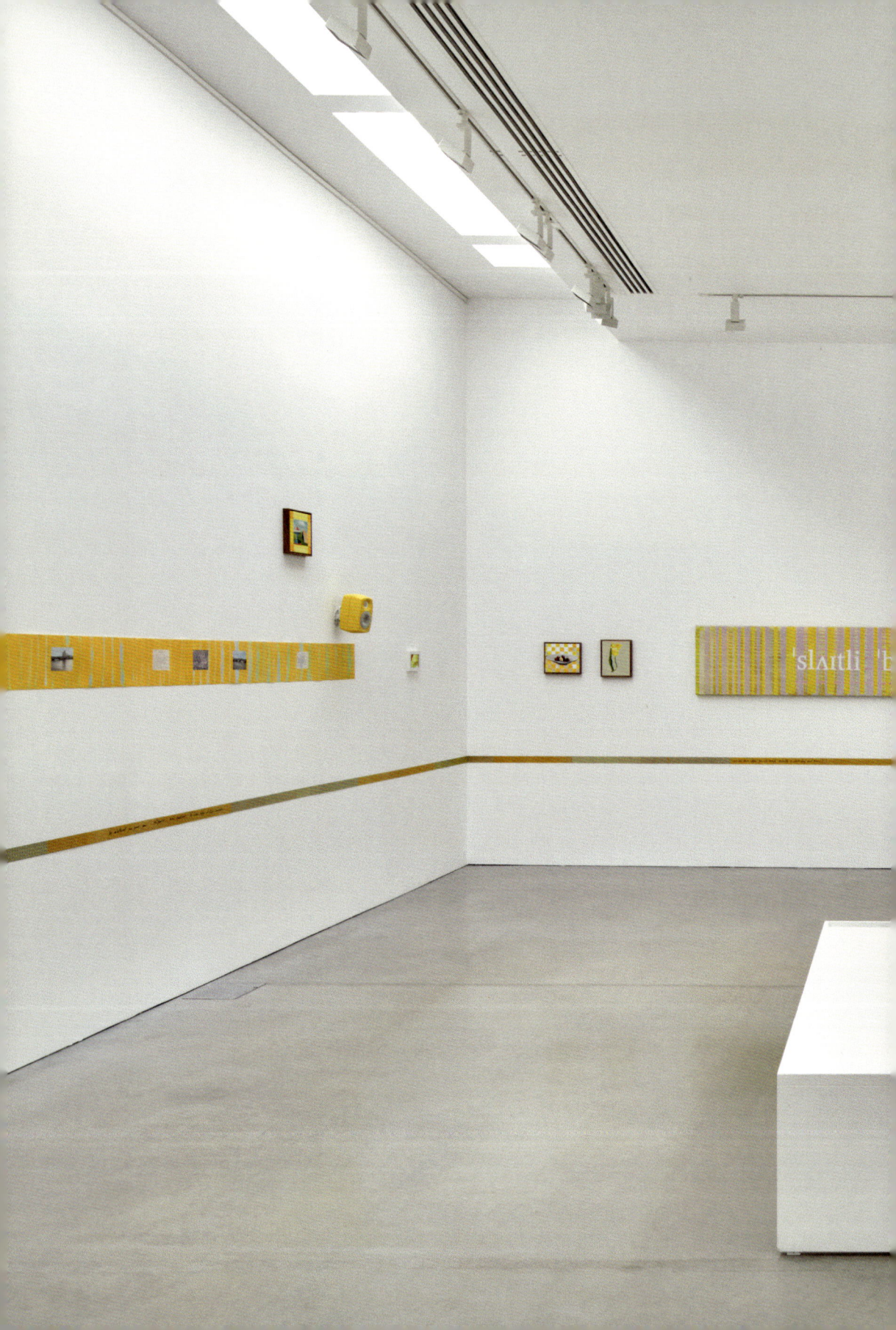

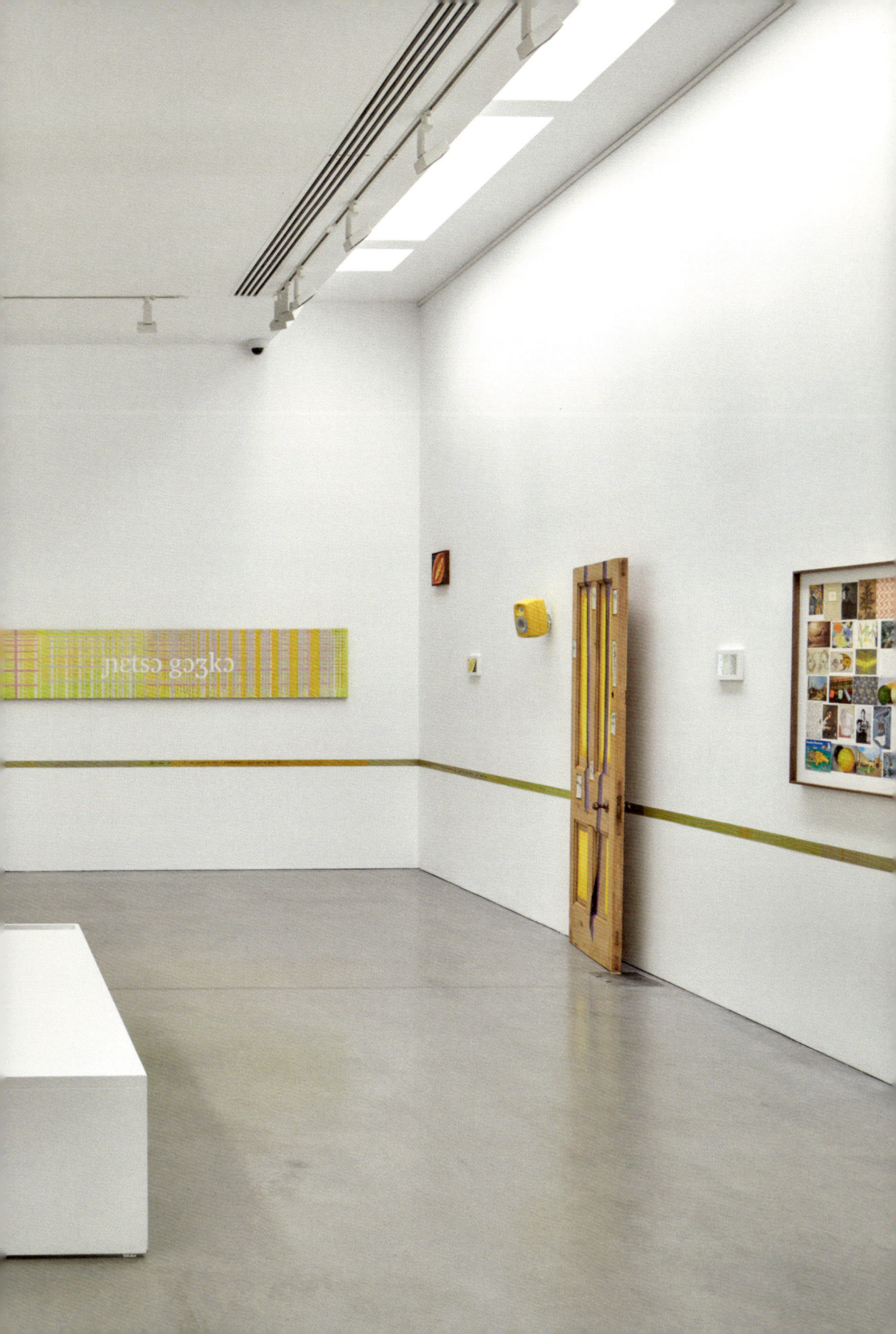

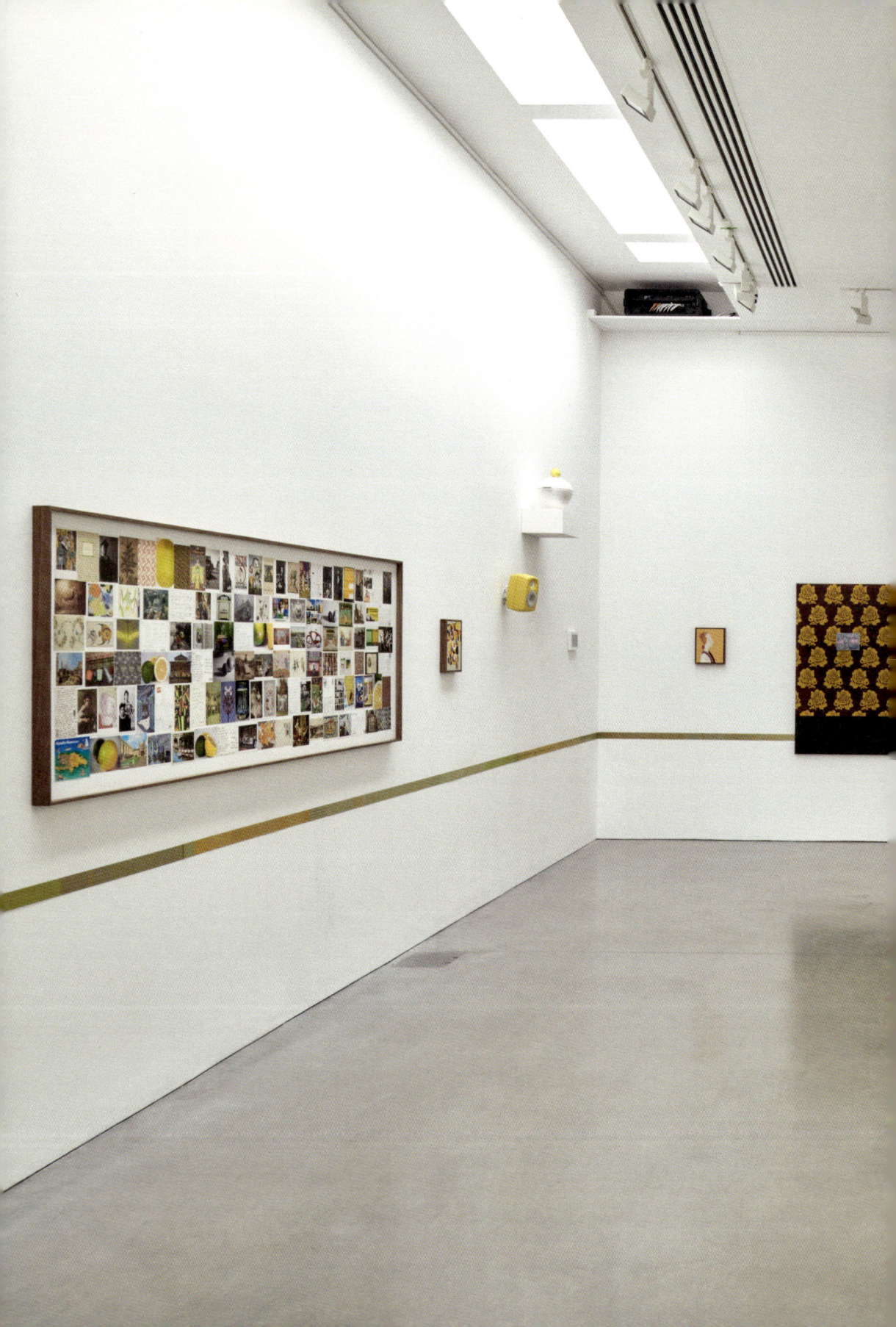

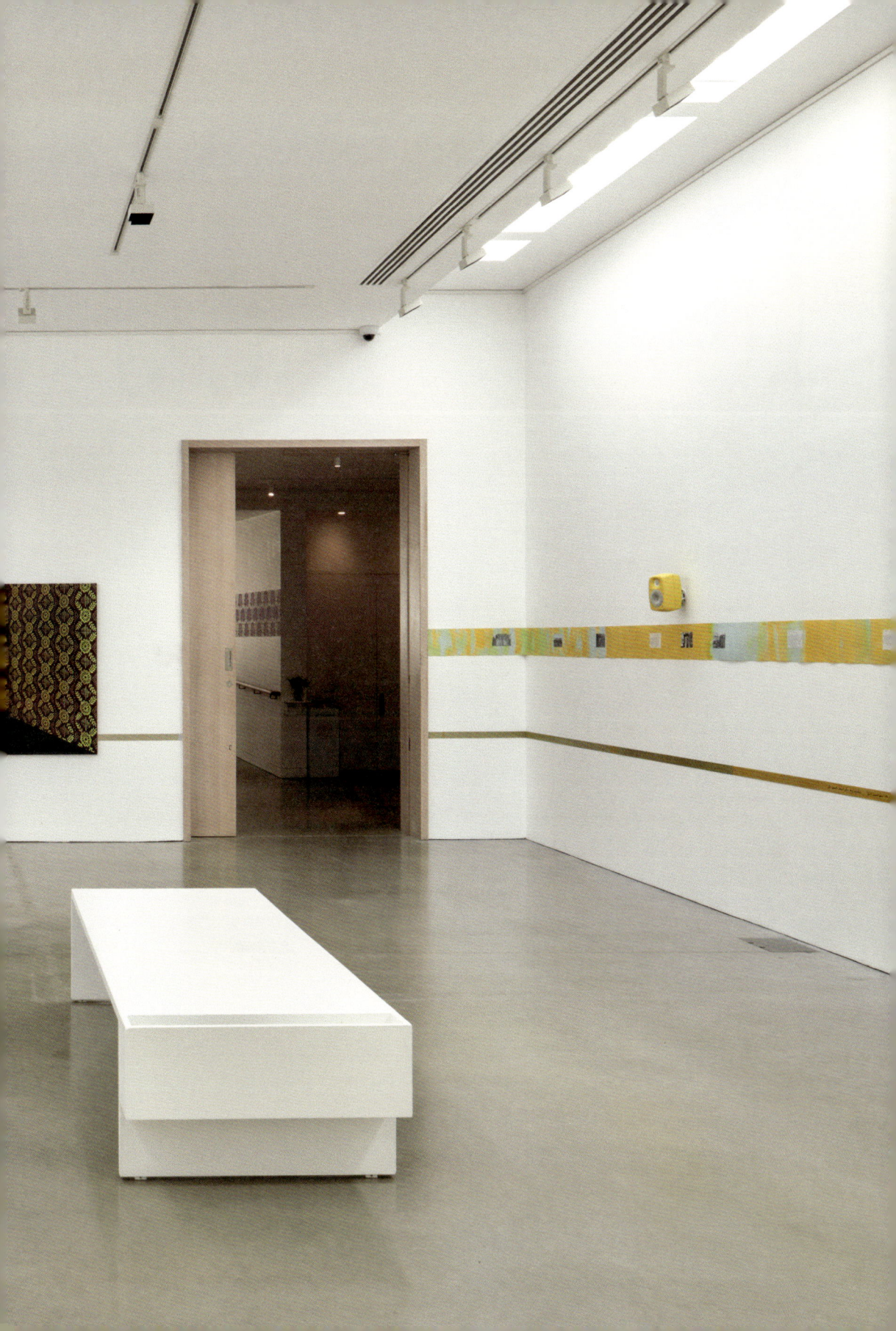

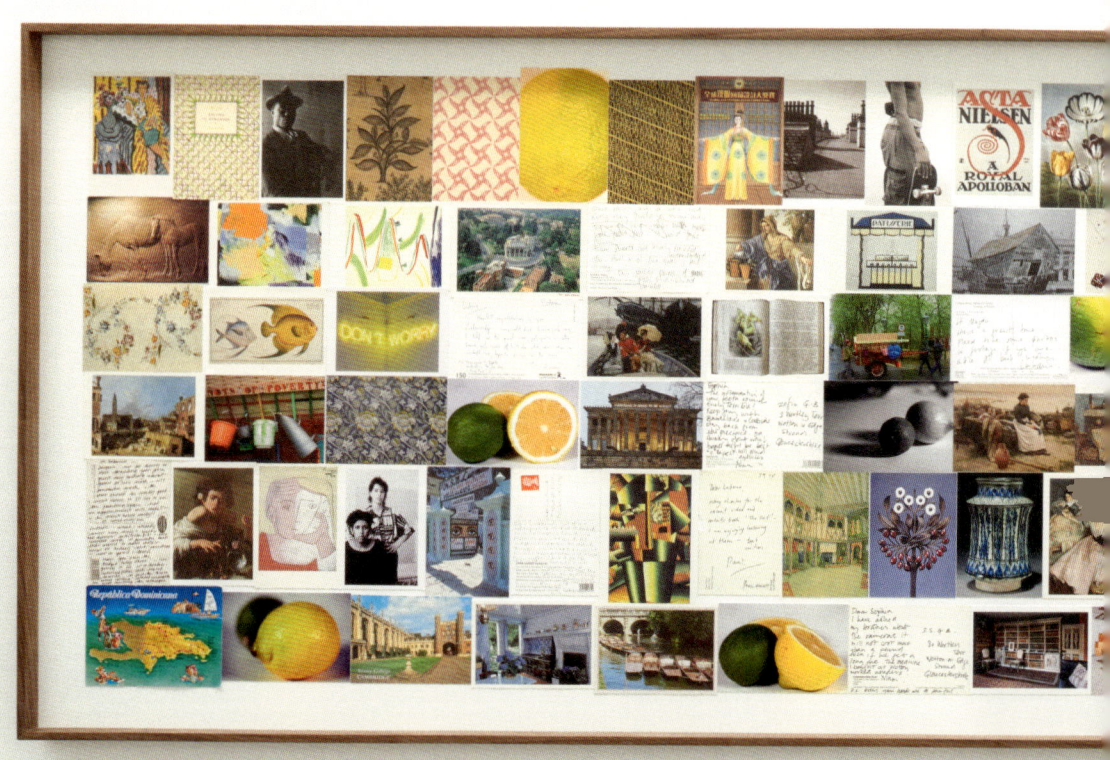

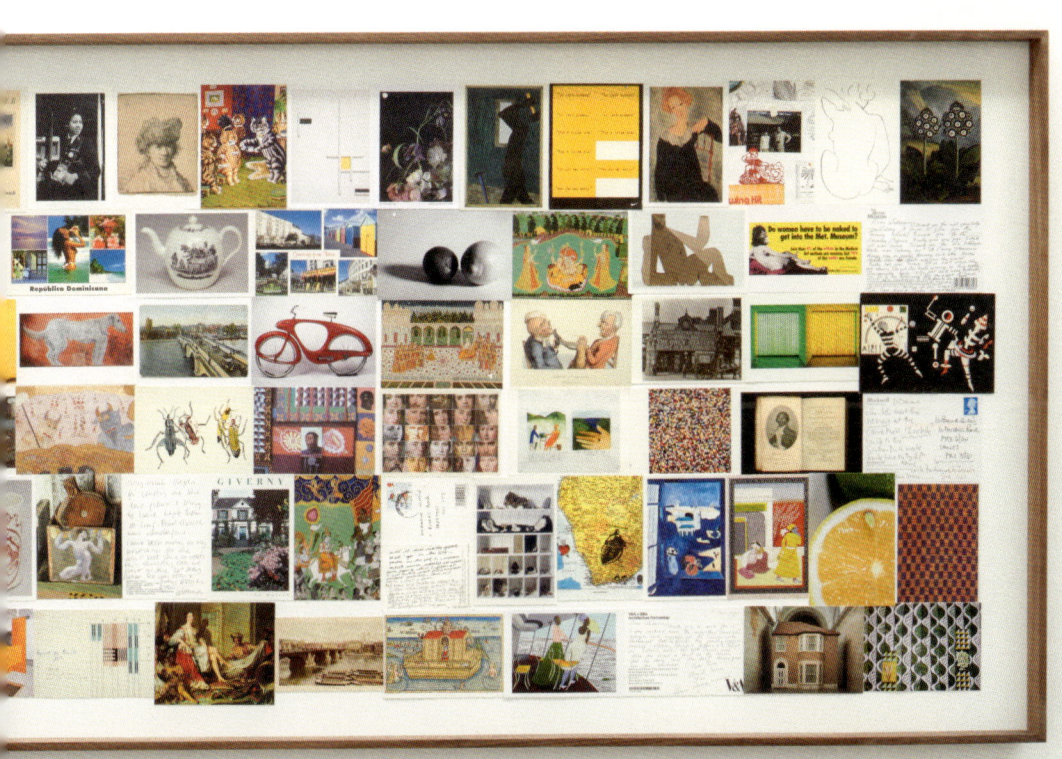

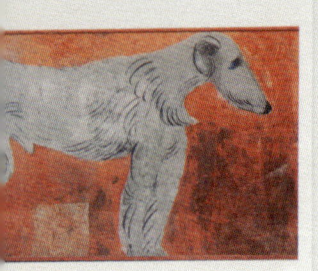

Dominicana

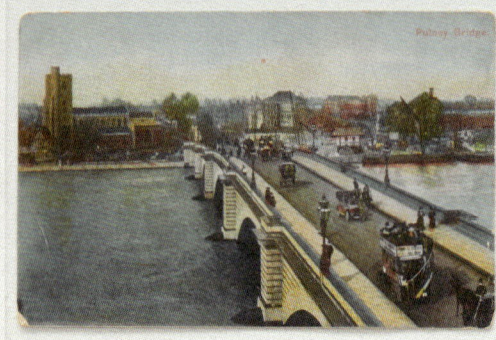

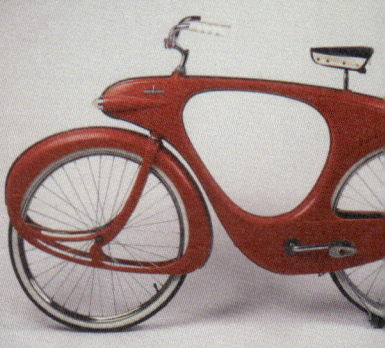

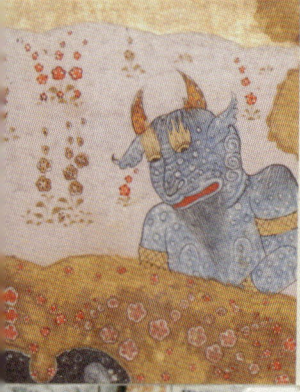

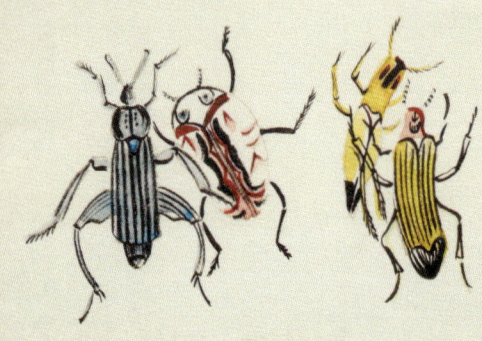

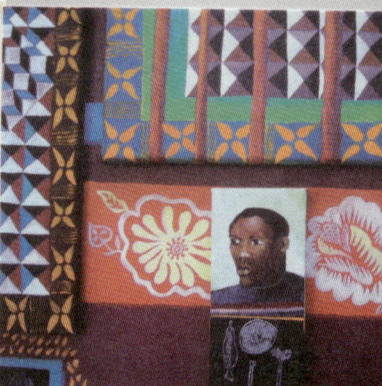

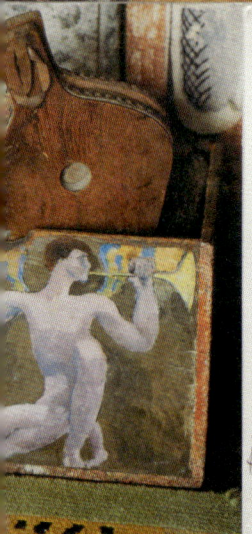

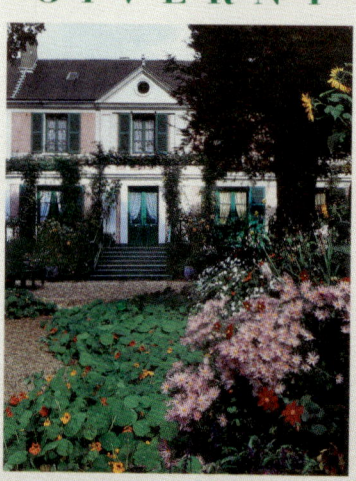

Many thanks Magda
for lending me the
two films & sorry
to have kept them
so long - Blind Chance
was wonderful -
I have been working on my
preparation for the
print but have to teach
this thursday. Can we
start on the 26th May
please. See you soon &
many thanks

GIVERNY

La maison

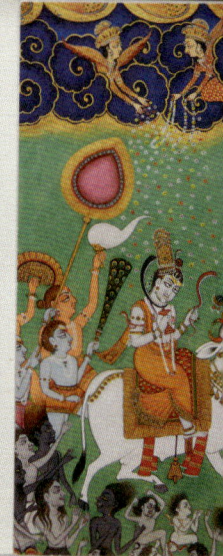

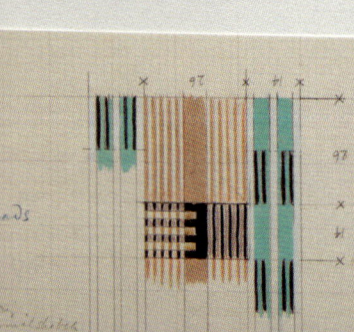

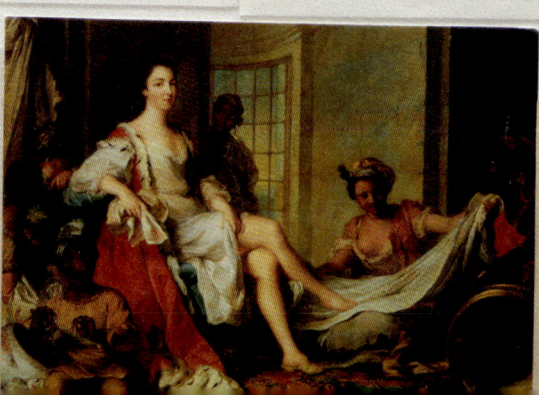

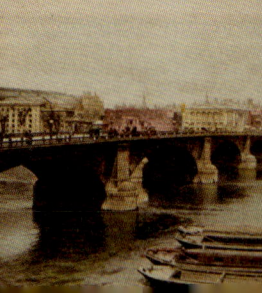

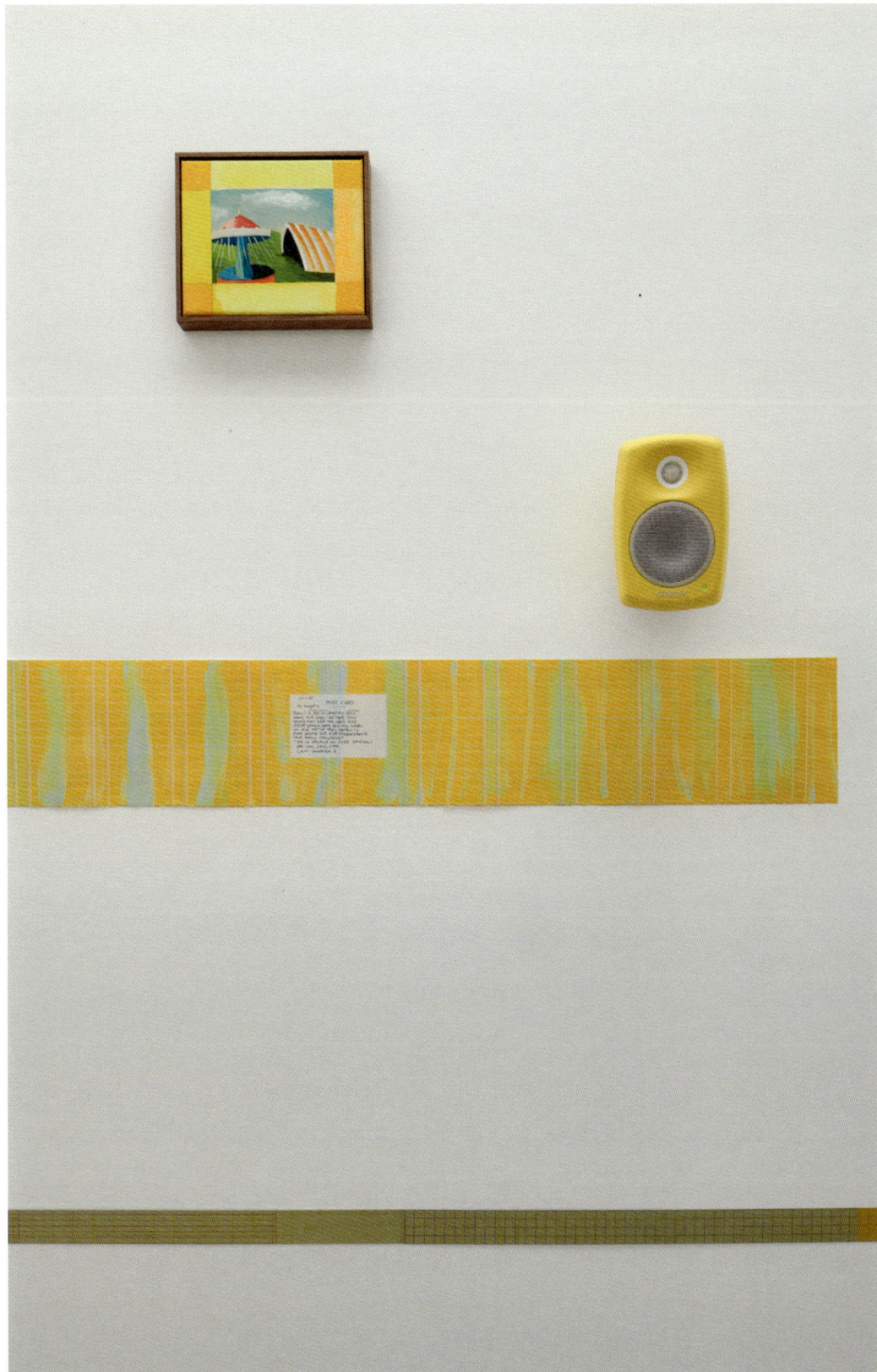

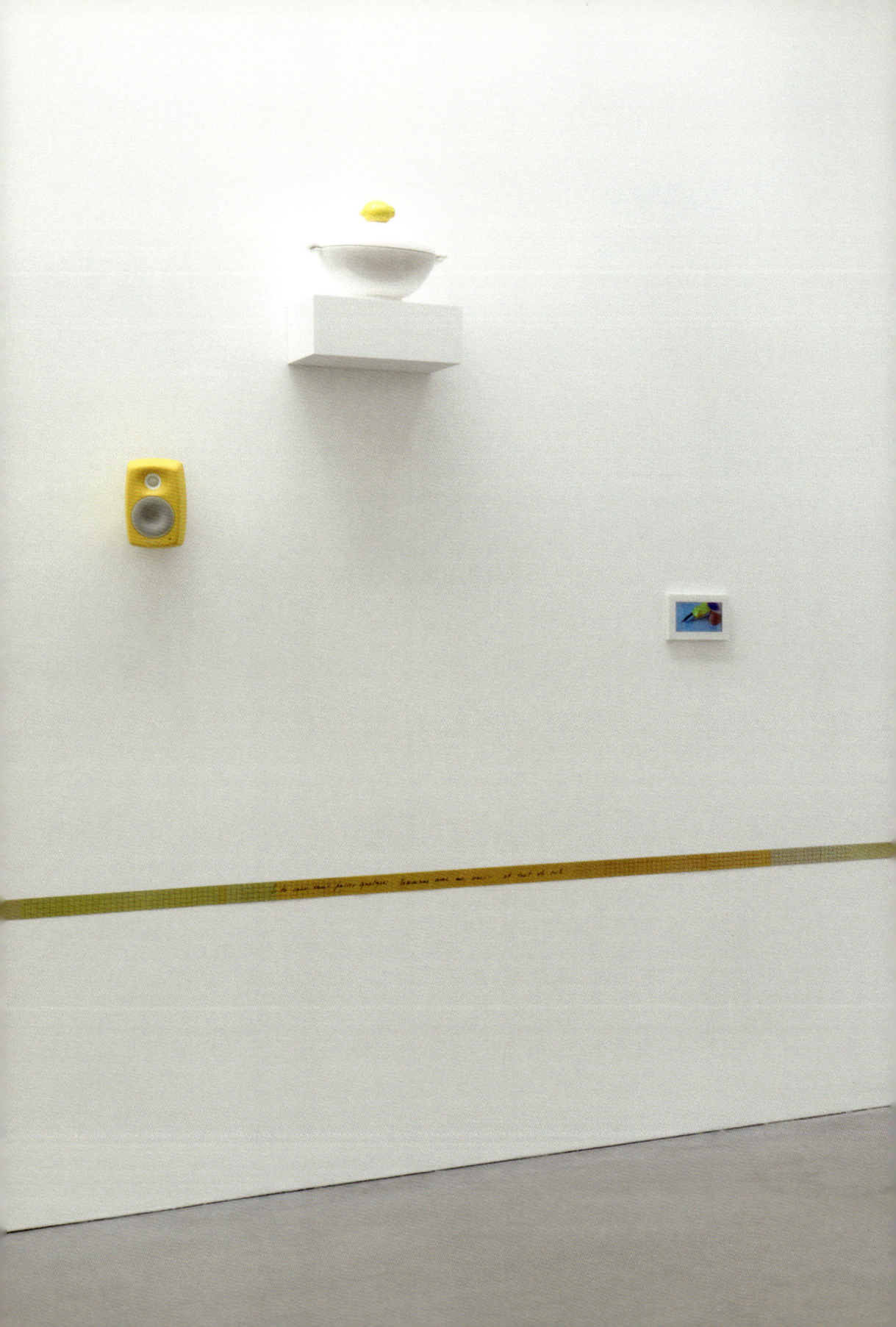

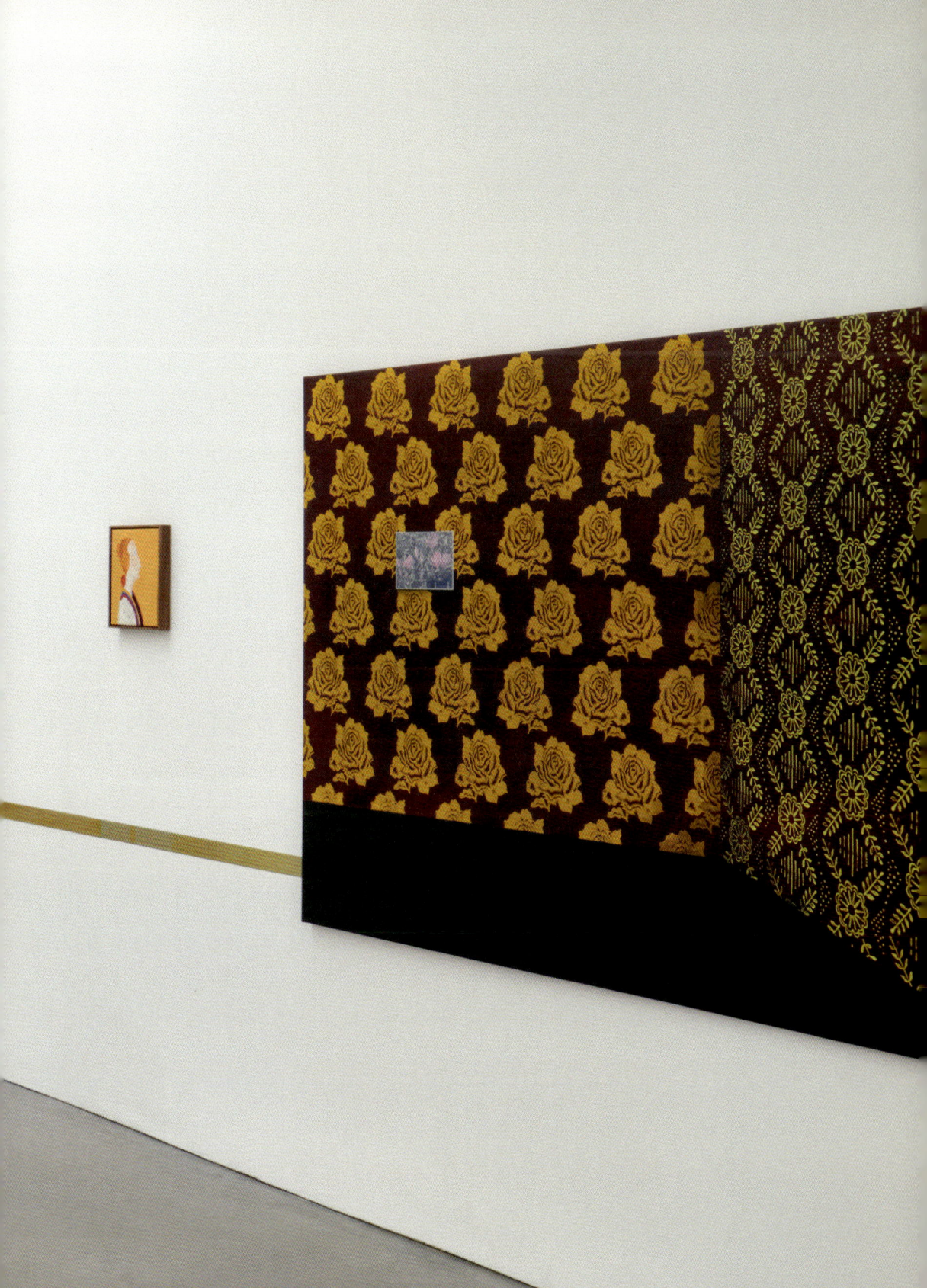

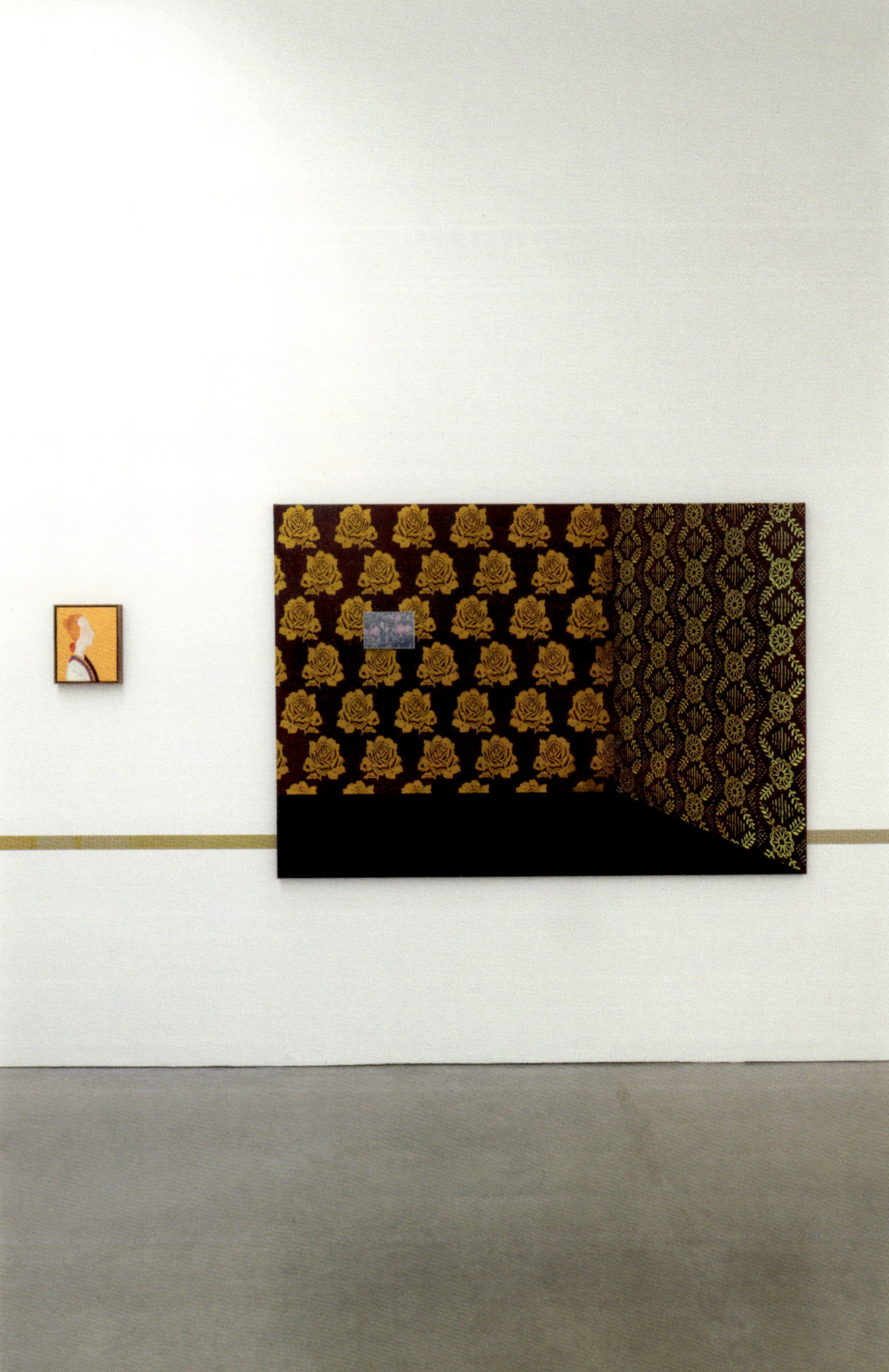

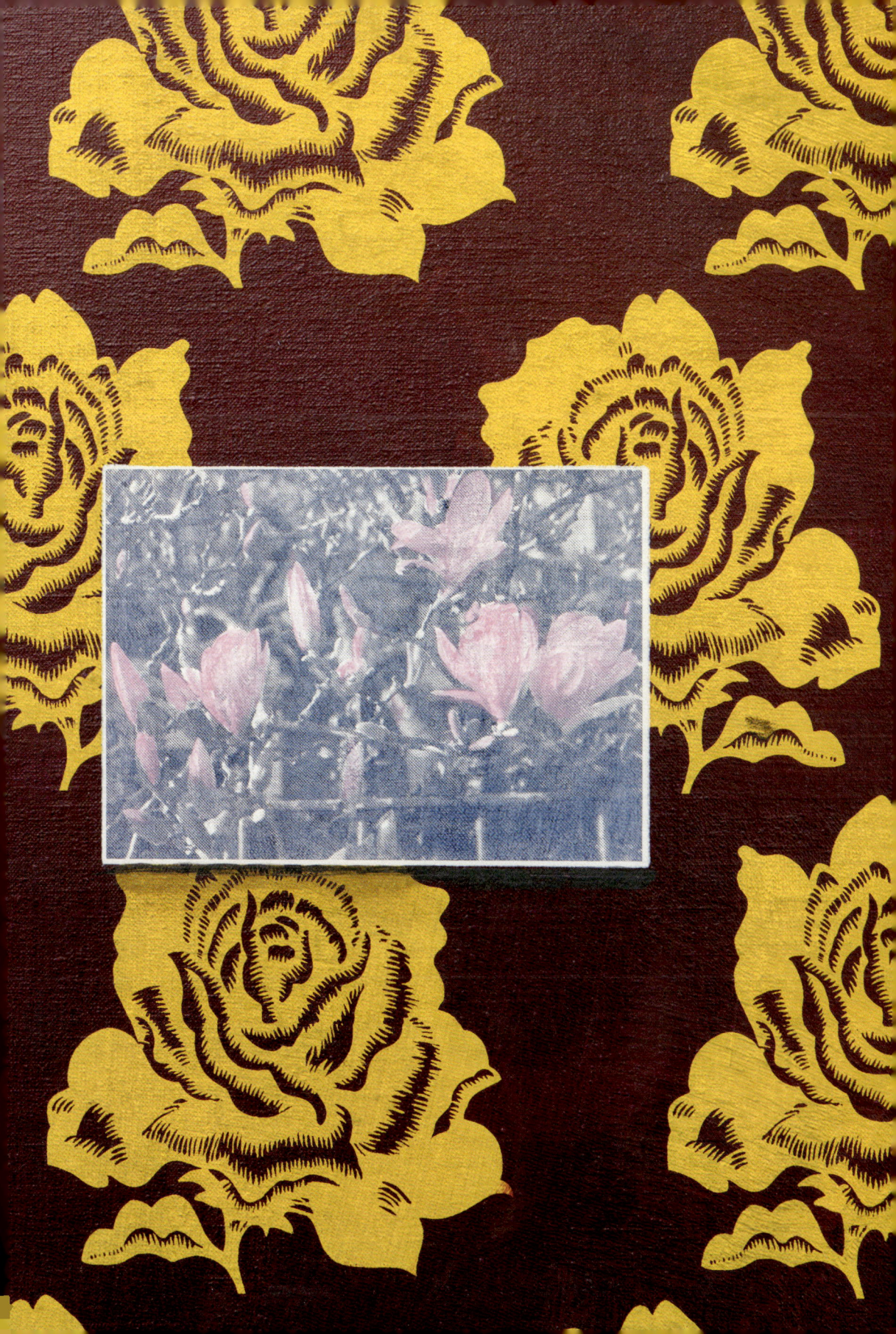

Thank you for your letter and for understanding my work
so well. I am very happy that we continue to speak
about everything and nothing to each other, even though
it's been twenty years since our paths crossed almost
by chance in the north of England.

I knew that you would understand why Lubaina and
I chose to work with the story of Zofia and Nina's
correspondence for the *Slightly Bitter* installation at
Kettle's Yard. I am really glad you found time to read
Zofia's book, *Matka*. It is amazing how, although she
died 100 years ago, her experiences of the reality of
being an immigrant, part of the Polish diaspora, feel
so relevant to us both.

I have chosen to use your voice alongside mine
and Lubaina's for the sound composition in the
installation. Although Zofia wrote letters and
postcards to Nina in English and French, I decided
that introducing her mother tongue would bring another
dimension to how those languages formed her identity
and ways of expressing herself. Do we feel more
deeply in our mother tongue? I am enjoying some of the
sentences in the English version of her letters, which
sound as if they were directly translated from Polish
idioms into English.

I layered your voice, speaking natural Polish and
French, with Lubaina's perfect received pronunciation
and my accented English. I am still fascinated by how
musical a language can sound even when one does not
understand it. It's astonishing how difficult it can be
to pronounce those unfamiliar phonemes; the shibboleth
which will almost always identify us as not belonging.

I am looking forward to showing you around Kettle's
Yard,

    Love,
    Magda

Hello Lubaina,

Thank you for thinking about our joint practice and for inviting me to collaborate on *Slightly Bitter* at Kettle's Yard. Yes, our starting point is the correspondence between Zofia and Nina, but the focus is on our conversations about how important small exchanges can be. A short letter or a postcard with a note of support or information can nurture a relationship, bringing two people together for a moment, or even for decades.

This is a real development from *Blue Grid Test* because, in this installation, we are both contributing visual elements – grids on metal, paper, and linen, our patterns one on top of another, my photographs interspersed among our postcards. Our texts are handwritten on my prints. Your tureen, my paintings, your door and my moving image work are being enveloped by the sound composition. A selection of extracts from their letters can be heard in our voices. The tones, colours and accents, yours so distinct from mine, are layered using our different languages. It's a sonic exchange, somehow, of all those things we talk about all the time in our joint quest to 'negotiate the unbelonging' in the everyday.

  Love,
  Magda

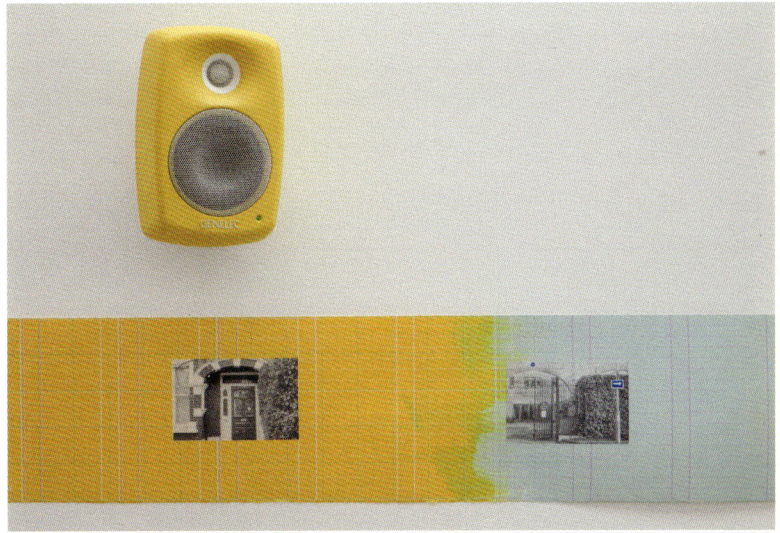

Magda Stawarska and Lubaina Himid, *Slightly Bitter* (detail), 2025

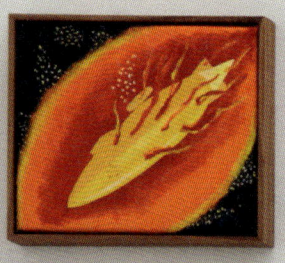

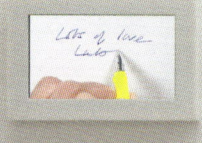

Afterword

We are immensely grateful to all those who have contributed to both the making of this book and the exhibition at Kettle's Yard. This publication benefits from insightful writing by Amelia Groom and Aneta Krzemień; special texts by Lubaina Himid and Magda Stawarska; and Mark El-khatib's outstanding design skills, also evident in his equally sensitive approach to creating the exhibition identity.

The generous support of the Another Chance Encounter Supporters Circle has been vital. Our thanks to: Alexander V. Petalas, Ali Smith and Sarah Wood, Andrew and Fiona Blake, Carlos and Francesca Pinto, Carol Atack and Alex van Someren, Kemal Has Cingillioglu, Edmund Hubbard and Nicole Bellamy, Emma Davis, Forster Foundation, Mandarin Trust, Nicholas Crompton, Porthmeor Fund, Sabine Jaccaud, Tamsin and Stewart Wilkinson and those who wish to remain anonymous.

We have benefited immensely from the help and advice of Hollybush Gardens, Himid's London gallery, who have championed her work over many years. Our warmest appreciation to Lisa Panting and Malin Ståhl, as well as to Grace Storey and Nella Franco. We are also grateful to Yamamoto Keiko Rochaix Gallery, who represent Stawarska, and Carol Greene, of Greene Naftali, Himid's gallery in New York.

The team at Kettle's Yard have been extraordinary. Especial thanks to Tom Allin-Roberts, Megan Breckell, Nastasha Boyce, Meri Croft, Beth Darbyshire, Helen Davies, Inga Fraser, Guy Haywood, Holly Kavanagh, Tom Noblett, Steven Penney, Laura Pryke, Ruby Salter, Karen Thomas, and Alison Waterhouse. It has also been a pleasure to work alongside members of Himid's studio team: Tao Lashley-Burnley, Chris Davison and Beth Hughes, as well as Kyle Partridge from ArtAV. Their expertise and dedication have been essential to achieving all aspects of an ambitious multi-layered project.

Our most heartfelt gratitude is reserved for Lubaina Himid and Magda Stawarska. They have produced an exceptional exhibition that extends across Kettle's Yard, encompassing the galleries, research space and house. In addition, a series of five vibrant banners by Himid, based on unexhibited paintings, are displayed in the Meadows Community Centre in Cambridge. Our thanks to Rachal Creek, Dan Mitchell and all at the Centre who have worked with us. As part of this project, Himid has invited shopkeepers to request one of the banners to be made into a curtain for their shop.

The curiosity central to Himid and Stawarska's art is only heightened by the commitment, insight and warmth they have brought to Kettle's Yard and our collaboration. Everything has been made with sophistication and wit, engaging visitors in the artists' telling of fictional and real stories. They enable us to see, speak and imagine not only more about Kettle's Yard, but how alternative histories and a renewed awareness of the present shape all our futures.

Andrew Nairne, Director
Amy Tobin, Curator, Contemporary Programmes

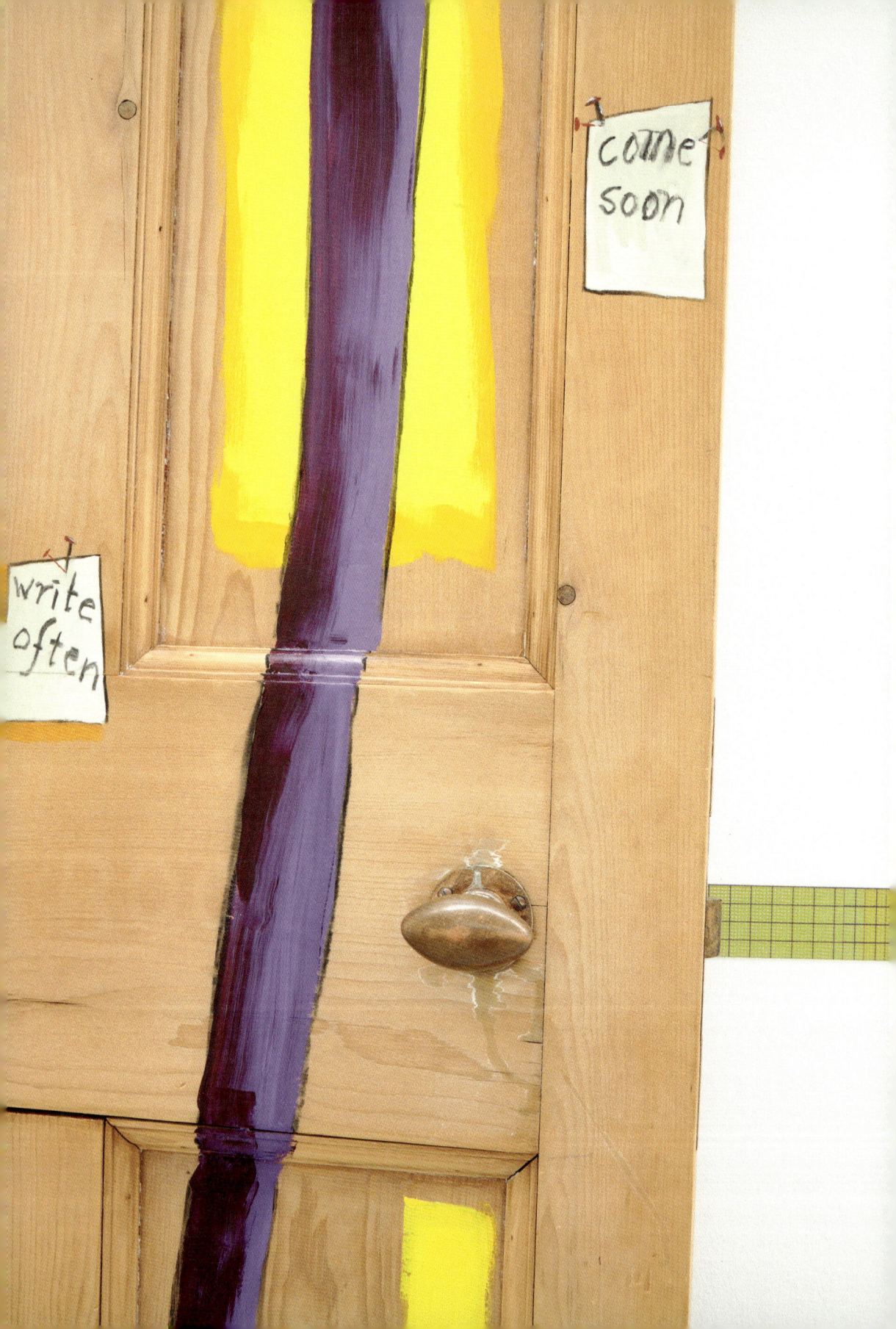

Collaborative Projects by
Lubaina Himid and Magda Stawarska

Slightly Bitter
Installation
Kettle's Yard, Cambridge, UK
Exhibited in *Lubaina Himid
with Magda Stawarska:
Another Chance Encounter*,
12 July – 2 November 2025

Nets for Night and Day
Exhibition
MUDAM, Luxembourg -
Museé d'Art Moderne
Grand-Duc Jean,
7 March – 24 August 2025

Street Sellers, 2024
Installation
Greene Naftali, New York,
USA, 2 May – 15 June 2024

Alla Prima/Cross Hatch
Print series
Cristea Roberts, London,
UK, 10 March – 22 April
2023

Plaited Time / Deep Water
Exhibition
Sharjah Art Foundation,
Sharjah, United Arab
Emirates, 29 October
2023 – 28 January 2024

Zanzibar, 1999–2023
Installation in *Rewinding
Internationalism: Scenes
from the 1990s, today*,
Van Abbemuseum, Eindhoven,
Netherlands, 19 November
2022 – 30 April 2023

*Airmail Letter: Notes on
a Blue Grid Test*, 2022
Installation
Shown in *Lubaina Himid:
Water Has a Perfect
Memory*, Hollybush Gardens,
London, 4 March –
30 April 2022

Blue Grid Test, 2020
Installation
Risquons-Tout,
WIELS Contemporary Art
Centre Brussels, Belgium,
12 September 2020 –
28 March 2021
Tate Modern, London, UK,
25 November 2021 –
2 October 2022
Musée Cantonal Des Beaux-
Arts, Lausanne, France,
4 November 2022 –
5 February 2023

*Reduce The Time Spent
Holding*, 2019
Old Boat/New Money, 2019
Shown in exhibition *Work
from Underneath*, 26 June –
6 October 2019
New Museum, New York, USA

*Naming the Money
(Soundtrack)*, 2017
Digital audio composition,
63 min
Shown in *Navigation
Charts*, Spike Island,
Bristol, 20 January –
26 March 2017

Front & Back Cover
Magda Stawarska and Lubaina Himid, *Slightly Bitter*, 2025 (details)
Courtesy Hollybush Gardens, London, Greene Naftali, New York and Yamamoto Keiko Rochaix Gallery, London.

pp. 2-4
Magda Stawarska, untitled print for Kettle's Yard, 2025 (details)
Digital print
Courtesy Yamamoto Keiko Rochaix Gallery, London.

p.6
Lubaina Himid, *Your Charm Offensive*, 2025 (detail)
From the series *How Can I Help You?*
Acrylic and charcoal on linen
Photo: Gavin Renshaw
Courtesy Hollybush Gardens, London and Greene Naftali, New York.

p. 10
Lubaina Himid and Magda Stawarska, *Zanzibar*, 1999-2023
Installation view *Nets for Night and Day* at MUDAM Luxembourg Luxembourg - Musée d'Art Moderne Grand-Duc Jean 7 March – 24 August 2025
Photo: Marc Domage
Courtesy Hollybush Gardens, London, Greene Naftali, New York and Yamamoto Keiko Rochaix Gallery, London.

p. 17
Lubaina Himid, *Favours for Years to Come*, 2025 (detail)
From the series *How Can I Help You?*
Acrylic and charcoal on linen
Photo: Gavin Renshaw
Courtesy Hollybush Gardens, London and Greene Naftali, New York.

pp. 21 & 22
Magda Stawarska and Lubaina Himid, *Slightly Bitter*, 2025 (details)
Courtesy Hollybush Gardens, London, Greene Naftali, New York and Yamamoto Keiko Rochaix Gallery, London.

pp. 26-27
Lubaina Himid, *Flying Carpet*, 2025
Acrylic and charcoal on linen
Installation view, Kettle's Yard, upper extension, *Another Chance Encounter*, 12 July – 2 November 2025
Courtesy Hollybush Gardens, London, and Greene Naftali, New York.

p. 28
Magda Stawarska, *Sweet Sharp Taste of Limes*, 2025
Sound installation
Installation view, Kettle's Yard, kitchen, *Another Chance Encounter*, 12 July – 2 November 2025
Courtesy Yamamoto Keiko Rochaix Gallery, London.

p. 29-31
Lubaina Himid, *Saving It For Later*, 2025
Acrylic on wall
Installation view and details, Kettle's Yard, cottages
Courtesy Hollybush Gardens, London, and Greene Naftali, New York.

pp. 32-33
Lubaina Himid, *Jelly Mould*, 2010
Painted ceramic
Installation views, Kettle's Yard library, *Another Chance Encounter*, 12 July – 2 November 2025
Courtesy Hollybush Gardens, London, and Greene Naftali, New York.

pp. 34-35
Lubaina Himid, *Man in a Swiss Army Drawer*, 2025
Collage and painting on found wood
Installation view, Kettle's Yard upper extension, dining table, *Another Chance Encounter*, 12 July – 2 November 2025
Courtesy Hollybush Gardens, London, and Greene Naftali, New York.

109

pp. 36-37
Magda Stawarska, *Cytrony*, 2025
Screenprint on Japanese paper
Installation view, Kettle's Yard
lower extension, *Another Chance
Encounter*, 12 July –
2 November 2025
Courtesy the artist and Yamamoto
Keiko Rochaix Gallery, London.

p. 41
Lubaina Himid, *Flying Carpet*, 2025
Acrylic and charcoal on linen
Photo: Gavin Renshaw
Courtesy Hollybush Gardens,
London, and Greene Naftali,
New York.

p.42
Lubaina Himid, *Naming the Money*,
2004
90 cut-out figures: plywood,
acrylic, mixed media and audio
Installation view, Spike Island,
Bristol, 20 January – 26 March
2017
Photo: Stuart Whipps
Courtesy Hollybush Gardens,
London, Greene Naftali, New York
and National Museums Liverpool.

pp. 46-47
Lubaina Himid, *How Can I Help
You?*, 2025
Installation views, *Another
Chance Encounter*, 12 July –
2 November 2025, Kettle's Yard,
Cambridge
Courtesy Hollybush Gardens,
London, and Greene Naftali,
New York.

p. 48
Lubaina Himid, *Their Elegance
Will Astonish You*, 2025
From the series *How Can I Help You?*
Acrylic and charcoal on linen
Photo: Gavin Renshaw
Courtesy Hollybush Gardens,
London and Greene Naftali,
New York.

p. 51
Lubaina Himid, *Favours for Years
to Come*, 2025
From the series *How Can I Help You?*
Acrylic and charcoal on linen
Photo: Gavin Renshaw
Courtesy Hollybush Gardens,
London and Greene Naftali,
New York.

p. 52
Lubaina Himid, *Repair Jobs*, 2025
From the series *How Can I Help You?*
Acrylic and charcoal on linen
Photo: Gavin Renshaw
Courtesy Hollybush Gardens,
London and Greene Naftali,
New York.

p. 55
Lubaina Himid, *Your Charm
Offensive*, 2025
From the series *How Can I Help You?*
Acrylic and charcoal on linen
Photo: Gavin Renshaw
Courtesy Hollybush Gardens,
London and Greene Naftali,
New York.

p. 56
Lubaina Himid, *Try Out a Few of
Them*, 2025
From the series *How Can I Help You?*
Acrylic and charcoal on linen
Photo: Gavin Renshaw
Courtesy Hollybush Gardens,
London and Greene Naftali,
New York.

pp. 58-60
Magda Stawarska and Lubaina
Himid, *Slightly Bitter*, 2025
(details)
Courtesy Hollybush Gardens,
London, Greene Naftali, New
York and Yamamoto Keiko Rochaix
Gallery, London.

pp. 64-65
Lubaina Himid and Magda
Stawarska, *Blue Grid Test*, 2020
Acrylic on various supports,
six-channel sound installation
Installation view, *Risquons
Tout*, WIELS Contemporary Art
Centre Brussels, 12 September
2020 – 28 March 2021
Photo: Philippe De Gobert
Courtesy Hollybush Gardens,
London, Greene Naftali, New
York and Yamamoto Keiko Rochaix
Gallery, London.

p. 68
Magda Stawarska, *Ida*, 2024
Single channel video with stereo
sound projected onto fabric and
paper, and installed with fabric
and cut-out paper
Installation view, *Drift* at
Keiko Yamamoto Rochaix Gallery,
1 June – 6 July 2024
Photo: Alexander Christie
Courtesy Yamamoto Keiko Rochaix
Gallery, London.

p. 71
Magda Stawarska, *Littoral
Enfolding*, 2024, acrylic paint
on stretched linen in the
foreground, and *Drift Horizon
I*, 2024, silkscreen print on
wallpaper in the background
Installation view, *Drift* at
Keiko Yamamoto Rochaix Gallery,
1 June – 6 July 2024
Photo: Alexander Christie
Courtesy Yamamoto Keiko Rochaix
Gallery, London.

p. 74
Magda Stawarska, *Bracka 40*, 2020
Installation
Spaces and Moments at Keiko
Yamamoto Rochaix Gallery,
25 September – 28 November 2020
Photo: Alexander Christie
Courtesy Yamamoto Keiko Rochaix
Gallery, London.

p. 77
Magda Stawarska, *Oranienburger
Straße*, 2019
Painting on Silkscreen Print,
Somerset paper
Photo: Steve Tanner
Courtesy Yamamoto Keiko Rochaix
Gallery, London.

pp. 80-89
Magda Stawarska and Lubaina
Himid, *Slightly Bitter*, 2025
(details)
Courtesy Hollybush Gardens,
London, Greene Naftali, New
York and Yamamoto Keiko Rochaix
Gallery, London.

pp. 90-95
Magda Stawarska and Lubaina
Himid, *Slightly Bitter*, 2025
Installation views, *Another
Chance Encounter*, 12 July –
2 November 2025, Kettle's Yard,
Cambridge
Courtesy Hollybush Gardens,
London, Greene Naftali, New
York and Yamamoto Keiko Rochaix
Gallery, London.

p. 96
Magda Stawarska and Lubaina
Himid, *Slightly Bitter*, 2025
(detail)
Courtesy Hollybush Gardens,
London, Greene Naftali, New
York and Yamamoto Keiko Rochaix
Gallery, London.

pp. 97-100
Magda Stawarska and Lubaina
Himid, *Slightly Bitter*, 2025
Installation views, *Another
Chance Encounter*, 12 July –
2 November 2025, Kettle's Yard,
Cambridge
Courtesy Hollybush Gardens,
London, Greene Naftali, New
York and Yamamoto Keiko Rochaix
Gallery, London.

p. 101
Magda Stawarska and Lubaina
Himid, *Slightly Bitter*, 2025
(detail)
Courtesy Hollybush Gardens,
London, Greene Naftali, New
York and Yamamoto Keiko Rochaix
Gallery, London.

pp. 103-106
Magda Stawarska and Lubaina
Himid, *Slightly Bitter*, 2025
Installation views, *Another
Chance Encounter*, 12 July –
2 November 2025, Kettle's Yard,
Cambridge
Courtesy Hollybush Gardens,
London, Greene Naftali, New
York and Yamamoto Keiko Rochaix
Gallery, London.